NY Nov 2000

£12

THE DAY'S WORK

THE DAY'S WORK

Kipling and the Idea of Sacrifice

John Coates

Madison • Teaneck
Fairleigh Dickinson University Press
London: Associated University Presses

© 1997 by Associated University Presses, Inc.

All rights reserved. Authorization to photocopy items for internal or personal use, or the internal or personal use of specific clients, is granted by the copyright owner, provided that a base fee of $10.00, plus eight cents per page, per copy is paid directly to the Copyright Clearance Center, 222 Rosewood Dr., Danvers, Massachusetts 01923. [0-8386-3754-X/97 $10.00 + 8¢ pp, pc.

Associated University Presses
440 Forsgate Drive
Cranbury, NJ 08512

Associated University Presses
16 Barter Street
London WC1A 2AH, England

Associated University Presses
P.O. Box 338, Port Credit
Mississauga, Ontario
Canada L5G 4L8

The paper used in this publication meets the requirements
of the American National Standard for Permanence of Paper
for Printed Library Materials Z39.48-1984.]

Library of Congress Cataloging-in-Publication Data

Coates, John (John D.)
    The day's work : Kipling and the idea of sacrifice / John Coates.
    p. cm.
    Includes bibliographical references (p.   ) and index.
    ISBN 0-8386-3754-X (alk. paper)
    1. Kipling, Rudyard, 1865–1936—Criticism and interpretation.
2. Psychological fiction, English—History and criticism.
3. Didactic fiction, English—History and criticism. 4. Sacrifice
in literature. 5. Order in literature. I. Title.
PR4857.C66   1997
828'.809—dc21   97-12975
                                                                                CIP

PRINTED IN THE UNITED STATES OF AMERICA

For Carole and Charlotte

Contents

Acknowledgments	9
Introduction	13
1. Failure and Success of Civilizations in *Puck of Pook's Hill*	37
2. *Rewards and Fairies:* Thor and Tyr, Necessary Suffering, and the Battle against Disorder	47
3. *Rewards and Fairies:* Loyalty and Sacrifice	62
4. Religious Crosscurrents in "The House Surgeon"	76
5. The Redemption Theme in *Limits and Renewals*	83
6. The Limits of Knowledge: "The Eye of Allah"	100
7. Kipling's Valediction to Art: "Proofs of Holy Writ"	120
Bibliography	128
Index	134

Acknowledgments

Quotations from the works of Kipling appear by permission of A. P. Watt Ltd. on behalf of The National Trust. Acknowledgment is made to Bantam Doubleday Dell Publishing Group for U.S. permission to quote from *Limits and Renewals* and *Debits and Credits*. The author wishes to thank Professor Zohreh T. Sullivan and Cambridge University Press for permission to quote from *Narratives of Empire: The Fictions of Rudyard Kipling*. He is also grateful to the editors of several periodicals who have allowed him to use material from his own previously published articles. Acknowledgment is made to the editor of *The Modern Language Review* for permission to use "Memories of Mansura: The Tints and Textures of Kipling's Late Art in 'The Eye of Allah'," *MLR* 85, no. 3 (1990). The author would also like to thank the editor of *English Literature in Transition* for permission to use "Thor and Tyr: Sacrifice, Necessary Suffering and the Battle against Disorder," *ELT* 28, no. 1 (1986), and the editor of *The Kipling Journal* for permission to reproduce "Religious Cross-Currents in 'The House Surgeon'," *KJ* 45 (1978); "Failure and Success of Civilisation in *Puck of Pook's Hill*," *KJ* 47 (1980); "Proofs of Holy Writ: Kipling's Valedictory Statement on Art," *KJ* 61 (1987); "Duty and Sacrifice as Aspects of *Rewards and Fairies*," *KJ* 62 (1988); and "The Redemption Theme in *Limits and Renewals*," *KJ* 65 (1991).

THE DAY'S WORK

Introduction

It might be useful to define the critical premises and position adopted in this short study of Kipling's work. Such a definition would, in effect, also offer an explanation of the book's purpose. Recent Kipling criticism presents an interesting and idiosyncratic variant of what is, perhaps, the general academic and literary scene. As in the wider world, older types of intellectual inquiry and frames of reference retain a surprising vigor while being permeated by, and yielding prestige to, other more fashionable terminologies and concerns. In addition, Kipling studies are modified, or complicated, by the existence of the *Kipling Journal* and of the Kipling enthusiasts whose interests and attitudes that periodical represents. As a canonical author, Kipling is unusual in having a large and admiring public that is outside university departments of English literature and, to some extent, detached from prevailing critical formulae and assumptions. Kipling's position in this regard is not, of course, unique. Such periodicals as the *Chesterton Review* and the *Charles Lamb Bulletin* and the public that supports them provide analogies with this wider Kipling readership.

Some interesting recent work on Kipling continues older Formalist or New Critical concerns. John Bayley, Elliot L. Gilbert, Harry Ricketts, and other writers in the Kipling commemorative issue *of English Literature in Transition, 1880–1920* (29, nos. 1 and 2 [1986]) consider Kipling's texts as works of art whose ambivalence and subtle texturing are vehicles of a hidden truth or meaning. The recent collection published by Dent (see Kipling 1989) was chosen to emphasize Kipling's interest in craftsmanship and his self-conscious artistry. While *Kipling Considered,* edited by Phillip Mallett (1989), offers a wide variety of views, it is a conservative collection, resistant to literary theory. Contributions analyze individual literary texts (notably well-known conundrums like "Mrs Bathurst") to discover the secret at the heart of them and, in general, concern themselves with questions of form. Some of the most useful recent accounts of the contexts of Kipling's writing, such as Mark Paffard's *Kipling's Indian Fiction* (1989), which relates Kipling's Indian short stories to previous literary images and English cultural expectations, use little or none of the contemporary theoretical formulae.

In spite of the fact that older critical techniques and approaches persist and even flourish in Kipling studies, the field has been influenced by recent innovations in both subjects and language. Several scholars have produced stimulating discussions of Kipling's texts in terms of gender theory, imperialist discourse, and masculinist rhetoric. These writers share certain preoccupations. They approach Kipling's texts through the deconstructionist paradigm of disruptive revelations. The texts disclose emotional or ideological material that, in various ways, overturns or fragments the order the texts themselves have attempted to impose upon it. Such jarring, intransigent material, undermining the discourses of "manliness" or of empire, undermines, too, the texts' overt purpose, often that of demonstrating coping or healing. Sandra Kemp's *Kipling's Hidden Narratives* (1985) is perhaps the most sophisticated exploration of the ways in which Kipling's imagination relates to official discourses and ideology. However, such a mode of inquiry has been widely adopted by other critics, often without Kemp's awareness of nuance.

Nora Cook in *Kipling's Myths of Love and Death* (1989) treats "Mrs Bathurst" as the expression of a homosexuality its author could not openly face and such Indian tales as "The Strange Ride of Morrowbie Jukes" as indicating covert fears of sexual degradation. Miscegenation in such tales is a metaphor for yielding to one's own sexual urges. Zohreh T. Sullivan (1984) reads "The Brushwood Boy" as a failed attempt to descend into the unconscious mind. Kipling cannot face his hidden fears or heal the split in his psyche. J. McBratney sees women in Kipling's writing as the "other," a term borrowed from Edward Said. Subject to negative stereotyping, this "other" cannot be comprehended or reconciled. It must be disposed of, either by death or by some surrogate for death (McBratney 1990). For S. P. Mohanty, Kipling's stories for children, and notably *The Jungle Book*, register the racial features of British ideology. Such stories attempt unsuccessfully to conceal embarrassing facts that undermine the ideology, especially the existence of a poor and dispossessed group among the "natural" white rulers.

Introduction 15

One of the latest books on Kipling, Zohreh T. Sullivan's *Narratives of Empire* (1993) offers one of the fullest displays of current critical interests. Sullivan, above all, concerns herself with the disrupted text and with the inadvertent revelation that undermines the discourse that has been superimposed upon hidden material. Apart from its scholarship, her book has another value. It enshrines much of the programme and language that critics of the late 1980s and early 1990s have found useful and appropriate in discussing Kipling's work. These are the kinds of approaches that have enjoyed most prestige and types of questions that have seemed most worth asking in the last few years. Sullivan sees Kipling's texts as "marked by unnamed and unacknowledged longing, desire and fear" (1993, 1). The texts offer a "contradictory pattern of desire to be loved and to control" (2). Drawing explicitly on Edward Said and Homi Bhabha and, presumably, implicitly on Foucault, Sullivan proposes to explore the way in which "colonial authority and the colonial subject are both constructed out of deeply fragmented moments of hybridity where the self articulates the Other out of similarity and difference" (4). Her own object is

> to understand through Kipling's playfully and profoundly ambivalent narratives the larger imperial episteme or field of knowledge and to understand a way of knowing a world whose strategies of configuring race, gender and power in binary terms is still with us. (4)

In reading Sullivan one is aware of having reached a point where an emancipation is becoming an orthodoxy and where what passes for rebellion is turning into conformity. It is not that the underlying preoccupations and assumptions of *Narratives of Empire* are indefensible or untenable. They are often, incidentally, fruitful and are invariably intelligently argued. What is disconcerting is the way in which certain historical premises are offered simply as indisputable facts. Presumably they are dogmas that no emancipated mind can allow itself to question. Thus, for example, imperialism is seen as embodying the "story" (178) that J. A. Hobson and Lenin both knew. (After the events of the last few years it is curious to find the name of Lenin being invoked.) According to the "story" the imperial state requires a control of information and a "policing" of daily life. It "relies on exploitation to protect the interests of a dominant class" (178). Imperialism in its cultural manifestations is virtually a form of psychosis.

> The emptiness that is the sign of the lack or [*sic*] of the female is part of the gendered domination of colonial consciousness and culture. . . . It

> valorized the least humane parts of British political culture "de-emphasized speculation, intellection and *caritas* as feminine" . . . Kipling's fallen colonizers are cultural reminders of nineteenth century anxiety about the fluidity of sexual and racial Otherness, an anxiety that insulates itself by excluding that which is deviant, dirty and effeminate. (82–83)

It would be rash and unhelpful to characterize summarily the often complex causes and effects of recent critical methods and objectives. Even if one felt inclined, it would be even more foolish to condemn, out of hand, methodologies that are often highly nuanced and sophisticated. Terms like "political correctness" and "hermeneutics of suspicion" are the language of shop-soiled polemic rather than that of intellectual debate.

However, it is possible to have serious reservations about what has become a very common way of discussing Kipling. With some variations, recent critics use a model that often becomes formulaic. The model posits an opposition between official ideology and discourse, on the one hand, and the covert knowledge or emotional anxiety that threatens them, on the other. (It is, incidentally, curious that a critical language that often challenges and exposes "strategies of configuring" based on binary opposition should itself frequently rest upon a rigid opposition between the "Other" and "gender subjectivity and selfhood under siege"). There is a problem, too, in the assumption that the ideology and its discourse will invariably be too rigid and that suppressed, subversive longings will be too "unnamed and unacknowledged" (1) for any adaptation or accommodation to be possible. Cook, McBratney, Mohanty, and several other critics insist again and again on the *failure* of the texts' attempts of mediation between public discourse and private longing. Sullivan's account of Kipling's language is more flexible and adroit:

> I see it as a more dynamic, slippery and sometimes oppositional discourse which, while mimicking the various voices of its uneasy and half-denied ideology, yet questions official structures and raises the possibility of regressed and alternating rereadings of official imperial mythology. (10)

The critic does not appear to envisage the possibility of intelligent adaptation *within* the discourses and mythology of imperialism. For instance, Kipling's attempts to portray processes of healing, as in "The House Surgeon," are compensatory fantasies intended to disguise a problem that remains insoluble (139–40).

In spite of the undeniable success of prestigious and fashionable critical discourses and the value of the issues and questions critics who employ such discourses often raise in regard to Kipling's work, these terminologies have their weaknesses. Critics working within them often show impatience with the variety, idiosyncrasy, and awkward edges of the material being handled. Such scholars seem to wish to reduce an immensely complex record or a tangled skein of conflicting evidence to a few simple patterns. Seeking to achieve, or to assume the air of, hard-edged accuracy and to avoid what they see as sentimental or impressionistic, these recent critics need to interpret the ideology and history implicit in texts as wholly knowable systems. With an interestingly symptomatic impatience, Sullivan remarks that Kipling

> blurs the distinction between the dominators and the dominated by including priests from Chubara, carvers from Ala Yar, Jiwun Singh, the carpenter and Gobind the one-eyed story-teller within the intimate category of "mine own people." (1)

The fascinating surface detail of Kipling's texts (or, to use humanist terms, the variety of life his works embody) are devices to disguise trite patterns of class or race domination.

The fundamental defect of some recent Kipling criticism is that often accomplished examinations of tropes or narrative strategies are linked to certain historical assumptions so generally shared as to seem mandatory. After many insights by the way, critics' arguments march to certain conclusions that offer familiar matter for edification to a particular intellectual season or set. These political and historical assumptions and conclusions are restrictive and doctrinaire.

Granted that his view is accurate, we in Britain have certainly not reached the condition a distinguished American historian recently described:

> Even to suggest that Western civilization is a model worthy of emulation or that imperialism was not all evil, as I had ventured to do in my class room, triggers the automatic change of "ethnocentrism." (Pipes 1994, 72)

Careful reading of Sullivan and other recent critics, named and unnamed, who employ a similar methodology fails to unearth a single suggestion that

British rule in Indian was other than mere oppression or that the language that helped to sustain that rule was other than the exhibition of an unstable, disintegrating fraud.

Critics of this school do not always show sufficient awareness that the historical generalizations they incorporate into their analyses are widely questioned. According to this commonly employed model, "as Hannah Arendt and others contend," history "needs myths and legends in order to contain what otherwise could not bear examination" (Sullivan 1993, 7). Historians and statesmen "help to formulate legend, ideology and mythology" in order "to shore up the idealizing fantasies of a community" and to protect a culture against external reality. That "reality" invariably is one of social, cultural, and gender dominance and exploitation outside, and of psychological damage to those within, the ruling elite.

Much of this scheme is plausible enough. The popularity among many of these writers of Walter Benjamin's dictum that every great culture is a record of suffering signals what is, after all, a valuable recognition of the human costs of civilizations.

However, one might be excused for believing that recent critics of Kipling see only the cost and, unlike Benjamin, are blind to the civilization. Furthermore, by laying such stress on politics as ideology and myth-making these writers ignore the practical realities of wielding power—of government and administration. The work Kipling's characters perform, whether building bridges or relieving famines, is work with tangible materials producing tangible effects. Their world cannot be reduced to "discourse" and "ideology."

More broadly, writers of this school ignore the tragic ambivalences and imperatives of wielding power in any society known to recorded history. Of course, for them terms like "recorded history" are not acceptable. History is simply myth and ideology. Yet, their own model is itself a form of historical analysis and, oddly, they themselves appeal to historical scholarship, from time to time, in support of it. (Sullivan [1993, 178] invokes the eminent Marxist historian Eric Hobsbawm, for example.) They appeal to history while denying the possibility of historical objectivity. At the same time they expunge or ignore material that does not serve to sustain their theses.

The point is clearer if one compares these recent Kipling critics' historical model with the treatment of human suffering and the cost of civilization in great historians from Thucydides to Gibbon and beyond. In these

Introduction 19

magisterial writers of the past there is a sense of balance lacking in the historical excursions of current Kipling criticism. Outstanding studies of the corruption and disintegration of great power structures—studies such as *The Peloponnesian War* or *The Decline and Fall of the Roman Empire*—do convey an inescapable sense that the Athenian hegemony and the Roman Empire *were* great. The ideals and achievements recounted in Pericles' funeral speech are set against the massacre at Melos, the Peace of the Antonines against Commodus and Elagabalus.

It is worth recalling so obvious a fact only in order to emphasize how one-sided and disabling are the historical views many recent Kipling critics agree to offer on matters relevant to a reading of his texts on imperialism, the Edwardian ruling class, the pre-1914 sense of crisis, or on British rule in India.

The record of the British Raj offered in any standard work (say, Woodruff's *The Men Who Ruled India*) is one as tangled and tragic as anything Thucydides or Gibbon describes. The sheer difficulties of government and the exercise of power, the varieties of relationships between rulers and ruled, the mixture of motives, the strange blend of high ideals and accomplishment with corruption and cruelty, make the whole subject one of dizzying and intractable complexity. It is this complexity which the formulae of recent critics simply erases.

However, Sullivan's explanations of imperialism as "inspired by economic need and defeated by political reality" (1993, 7) or as "the chance for the Englishman to . . . play authoritarian parent, and re-write the failed family romance once again with England playing the role of a mythical Prospero . . . controlling a Caliban's Kingdom" (6) are *historical* explanations (or simplifications). Although such notions have become received opinion among a large and influential circle of contemporary literary critics, they remain hypotheses to be assessed by the degree to which they explain or interpret the available evidence.

To take a particular instance, Sullivan's view of the events of 1857–58 as "the return of the socially repressed in the form of Mutiny or Revolution" and "subsequently a source of uncanny shock that disturbs the social hierarchy psychically and provokes irrational responses" (2) sets aside, or simply ignores, a widely held serious view among many authorities. There is a body of scholarship that sees the Indian Mutiny much less as a national revolt than as a reaction of smaller landowners and religious leaders against what Sir James Outram (Morris 1979, 222) called the "crusading spirit of the past five and twenty years."* Confined to the Ganges plain and drawing virtually all its support from the recently annexed Kingdom of Oudh, it was the violent outburst of those who felt their privileges threatened. It is arguable that the spate of reforms beginning with the abolition of suttee (1829), followed by that of other forms of human sacrifice, and the replacement of a law code based on personal status by one applicable to all citizens (1837) had been precipitate. The Mutiny, on this view, was the desperate bid of a ruling group attempting to regain its power in an area with little direct experience of foreign rule and where the nature of British intentions were, consequently, most suspected. The call to revolt was entirely rejected by whole provinces and by entire social groups in India, notably by the educated middle classes in the great port cities.

To take another instance, Sullivan interprets the opening sentence of *Kim* as one that "allows two images to confront and collide against each other—the Gun and the Lahore Museum" (1993, 149); the gun is the emblem of British authority and the museum is the "Wonder House that is India." Yet Zam-Zammah the "fire breathing dragon" has a significance that goes far beyond a mere expression of power. Cast by a Moslem army from the loot of the captured city of Lahore (1757), it was used at the second battle of Panipat, the murderous climax of the wars between Hindu and Moslem that followed the disintegration of the Mogul Empire. It was, of course, this self-destructive clash between the Indian rulers that allowed the British to establish their Raj and that that Raj largely brought to an end. The image of the child playing on the old gun with which *Kim* opens affirms the achievement of that relative peace and security which is the condition of the "Wonder-house" of India rather than a power standing in opposition to it. It is important not to miss the nuances in this crucial opening image, since such implications are bound to influence the subsequent reading of the novel.

What weakens the otherwise talented work of some recent Kipling critics is that they state and argue in the fields of history and culture, but they do not discuss. In addition, their statements and arguments are often founded on ill-defined standards of comparison. Sullivan, McBratney, Mohanty, and their mentor Edward Said may well be correct in many of their observa-

---

*Such a view of the Indian Mutiny is offered in Singhal 1983, a recent standard textbook: "Whatever the character of the Revolt no one can deny that it was an attempt to revive the old feudal order. If the Indians had won there was hardly a chance of a democratic government and the development of a modern economy" (290).

tions about the dubious origins and damaging psychological effects of nineteenth-century imperialism. Yet one is entitled to ask how British India compares, in terms of the problems, achievements, and corruptions inherent in the exercise of power, with the two imperial predecessors on the subcontinent: the Moguls and the Sultanate of Delhi. It might be said that most readers know too little about these societies to make such a comparison. However, some information about them is readily available, which is more than can be said for the notional or not yet achieved values and social structures upon which judgments about gender stereotyping, masculinized discourse, disruptive encounters with the "Other," and so forth are being made. If not edited to fit a thesis, the past exists in enigmatic, puzzling, and inconsistent detail. The future is a blank wall on which one can inscribe any slogan or formula one chooses. Perhaps it is not ill-natured to find something faintly ridiculous in the spectacle of great empires, which have spanned centuries, covered countries, and ruled multitudes for good or ill, being condemned or dismissed in the (briefly) current catchphrases of some sheltered academic coterie.

The critical position and objectives of this book are influenced by what, I feel, is a certain lack of range, depth, and magnanimity in the historical frame of reference in which Kipling is often judged at present in some quarters. Saying this does not, of course, involve an equally one-sided partisan defense or rehabilitation of imperialism.

It might be worth recalling the reaction that J. A. Hobson's theses, developed by Lenin and used by Sullivan as an axiomatic historical basis for her argument, aroused, at the time when they were produced, in other critics of the British Empire. G. K. Chesterton made his reputation, initially, by a series of brilliant, hard-hitting attacks in *The Speaker* on the Boer War, on the financial speculations of the Rand millionaires, and on the cult of empire. His verdict on Hobson's fundamental failure of imagination and of generosity of mind is therefore all the more interesting and telling:

> I disliked Imperialism; and yet I almost liked it by the time that Hobson had finished speaking against it . . . I may be wrong; anyhow, I missed something, as he picked holes in the British Empire until it consisted entirely of holes tied together with red tape. And then Cunninghame-Graham began to speak; and I realised what was wanting. He painted a picture, an historical picture like a pageant of Empires, talking of the Spanish Empire and the British Empire as things to be reviewed with an equal eye; as things brave and brilliant men had often served with double

or doubtful effect, he poured scorn on the provincial ignorance, which supposes that Spanish Empire-builders or proconsuls had all been vultures of rapine or vampires of superstition; he declared that many of the Spanish, like many of the English, had been rulers of whom any Empire might be proud. And he traced such figures against the dark and tragic background of those ancient human populations which they had so often either served or conquered in vain. (1959, 248–49)

Perhaps one might say that the qualities Chesterton found wanting long ago in Hobson are wanted now in some recent Kipling critics.

The Chesterton passage is interesting for another reason. It gives a glimpse of an 1890s and Edwardian mood that is often encountered in Kipling's own writings, most memorably perhaps in "Recessional" and in "Cities and Thrones and Powers." It is a mood compounded of a melancholy sense of the passing of time, of a foreboding of the decline of the British Empire, and of an awareness of parallels between that decline and the waning of previous dominions and powers. Most readers of late-nineteenth- and early-twentieth-century literature will know the note well. It is struck in contexts that have become almost too familiar, such as the opening of *The Heart of Darkness,* or is implied in minor details such as the connotations of the statue of Charles IV in *Nostromo* (Conrad 1967, 52). It is found in popular fiction like Conan Doyle's "The Last Galley" with its picture of the rich, helpless Carthage being overwhelmed and its ominous epigraph "Mutato nomine, de te, Britannia, fabula narratur" (Doyle 1951). Transitory journalism, like Belloc's sketching (1912) of a stupid, money-grubbing Carthaginian aristocracy aimlessly chatting about upstart Rome, carries a similar meaning. Belloc's readers are meant to see parallels with Rand millionaires or Edwardian press barons and for Rome to read the German Empire. Contemporary reviewers often noticed similar concerns in Kipling. For instance, Alfred Noyes, discussing *Puck of Pook's Hill,* suggested that Kipling's portrayal of the "very deep pathos" of the failing energies of Roman soldiers on Hadrian's Wall might well imply that he "sees the writing on a certain modern wall" (1971, 300).

Various intellectual, philosophical, religious, economic, and political reasons have been offered to explain this widespread sense of melancholy historical patterns of decline. Such reasons are so familiar as to be part of the mental furniture of anyone who has made even a cursory examination of the period. It would be natural, for example, to refer to Max Nordau's *Degeneration* (English translation, 1895) whose "little parasitic paragraphs of small talk and scandal" (Shaw 1986, 340), abusing an assortment of late-nineteenth-century literary and artistic figures, achieved an enormous popularity. Meretricious as Nordau's book was, it ministered to a widespread feeling of living in an era of decline with analogues in other eras. In Nordau's view, it "is not for the first time in the course of history that the horror of world annihilation has laid hold of men's minds" (quoted in Thornton 1983, 9).

In the 1890s and 1900s the perennial cultural need to envisage social and moral degeneration in the age in which one lives coalesced with other fears. The bleak implications of evolutionary determinism joined with the dread of biological retrogression in the work of Galton and Lankester. "General" William Booth's *In Darkest England and the Way Out* (1890) portrayed the slums of great cities as torture chambers of the lost, while rural depopulation with the attendant disintegration of communities and traditions was the theme of Rider Haggard's *Rural England* (1902), to which Hardy contributed. "Father Time," the child in *Jude the Obscure,* devoid of either joy or curiosity, is a composite of many of these fears and perceptions of rural decay, of the failure of community and tradition, of evolutionary determinism.

The only point in recalling this well-known intellectual and emotional atmosphere is to remind ourselves of Kipling's place within it or his reaction to it. Current and often interesting critical inquiries into imperialist discourse and what it may have concealed and into what Sullivan calls "the cracks in the ideological structures that sustained the dreams of empire" divert attention from important and unignorable facts. Whatever their covert tensions and contradictions may have been, Kipling's texts acknowledge and, to a greater or lesser extent, were informed by an *overt* sense of danger, disintegration, demoralization, and possible chaos.

The existence of a widespread mood is clearly far more significant than a list of "pessimistic" late-nineteenth-century authors. One wants to estimate the popular cultural diffusion of "pessimism." How widespread was it? No final answer to such a question is possible. However, intelligent contemporary observers never doubted the existence and importance of such general despondency, whether as a loss of belief in the worth and aims of life or simply as blank ennui and sadness. In his *The Victorian Age in Literature,* a brilliant pioneering study of the history of ideas and of the cultural context of literature, Chesterton pointed to what he saw as the simultaneous failure of civic and religious hope:

> These years that followed on that double disillusionment were like one long afternoon in a rich house on a rainy day. It was not merely that everybody believed that nothing would happen; it was also that everybody believed that anything happening was even duller than nothing happening. (1947, 143)

Best-sellers and mass-readership fiction confirm the strength and existence of a popular mood more than do exceptional and outstanding literary texts. The novels of Henry Seton Merriman, now almost forgotten but so widely read in the 1890s, have been described as being

> much influenced by Fitzgerald's version of Omar Khayyam which came out of copyright at the end of the nineteenth century and was printed in various delightful forms—"The Moving Finger writes" etc. . . . And the moral is always that men should be brave, that women should be enduring, that the worldly hopes of human beings bring no satisfaction, and that the British are the salt of the earth. (Swinnerton 1966, xvi–xvii)

Recent critics have stressed Kipling's extreme reticence and his suppression of emotional material. Thomas Pinney's fine edition of Kipling's *Something of Myself and Other Autobiographical Writings* (1990), for example, stresses the factual economy and deliberate gaps in Kipling's account of his own life. Such reticence (arguably less extreme in the context of Kipling's social class and period) does lend itself to current preoccupations with the occluded, suppressed, or denied; with that which lies below the surface of and threatens to subvert official discourse and ideology. The secretive Kipling must have had a great deal to hide and what he was concealing must certainly have stood in contradiction to what he seemed to be saying, to the surface of his art:

> The dual plot of Kipling's life and art at its most vital involves a dialectic between the accurate, the official and the prescribed as against the dreamlike, the repressed and the outlawed. (Sullivan 1993, 30)

Kipling's guarded comments on his own life are modified by one's sense of his constant *open* concern with pain, disintegration, with loss of hope or meaning. For him, the private and public dimensions of these dangers were connected. They were a peril to individuals, to the ruling elite of which those individuals were members, and to the state such an elite administered and served. A speech entitled "Values in Life," given at McGill

University in 1907, is one of many examples of Kipling linking the private and public dimensions of prevalent temptations to despair. After warning his audience of future officers, administrators, and civil servants away from lives of paltry moneymaking smartness, "one of the most terrible calamities that can overtake a sane, civilised, white man in our Empire today," Kipling reaches the climax of his speech:

> They say youth is the season of hope, ambition and uplift—that the last word youth needs is an exhortation to be cheerful. Some of you here know—and I remember that youth can be a season of great depression, despondencies, doubts, waverings, the worse because they seem to be peculiar to ourselves and incommunicable to our fellows. There is a certain darkness into which the soul of the young man sometimes descends—a horror of desolation, abandonment, and realised worthlessness, which is one of the most real of the hells in which we are compelled to walk. I know of what I speak. (1928, 19–20)

This long-standing concern with pain and loss of meaning, public and private, overlaps but is not identical with familiar themes of breakdown and forgiveness in late stories, such as "Dayspring Mishandled" and "The Gardener," which have sometimes been taken to mark a radical change in Kipling's work brought about by the First World War.

In fact, Kipling's concern to teach, to heal, and to make life bearable was markedly present from a much earlier stage in his career. His well-known contempt, as a young man in literary London, for posturing aesthetes, the "long-haired things . . . Who talk about the Aims of Art" (Carrington 1970, 187), was clearly far from being a contempt for high aims in art, as such. The point of such attacks on contemporary views of art was that such views were weak and parasitic, devoid of a social function or a sense of social purpose. "Tomlinson," in the satirical poem of that title (Eliot 1973, 146–53), has "read . . . heard . . . thought . . . felt . . . guessed" and nourished his mind with what reviewers have said about what other critics have written about Tolstoy or Ibsen. (The poem's reference to these two authors as "a Prince of Muscovy" and a "Karl of Norroway" is an alienating device that stresses the fact that such culture as Tomlinson's is thin, third-hand gossip about remote and outlandish figures.) Even Tomlinson's act of adultery is intertextual, something he has read about in a book and imitated. Like the souls in Dante's vestibule of Hell, he refuses creative or even authentically destructive choice and is unworthy of damnation as much as of salvation.

Kipling's early verse contains numerous declarations of explicit purpose in his writing, and, by implication, of suggestions about the nature and value of art in general. One of art's most important purposes is the transfiguring of "ordinary" experience. Homer in "When 'Omer Smote 'is Bloomin' Lyre" drew his poetry out of what he "stole" from "market-girls and fishermen." Shakespeare in "The Craftsman" (143, 146) stands in contrast to "overbearing Boanerges Jonson's" cultural and scholarly pretensions. (It was a contrast Kipling was to develop at the very end of his career in "Proofs of Holy Writ.") In Kipling's early poem, the figures in Shakespeare's tragedies are drawn from mundane material. Cleopatra is based on an ale-wench's "enormous, salvation-condemning" love of a tinker and Lady Macbeth on a "sombrely scornful" seven-year-old girl who drowns kittens while her brother flinches.

As Mark Paffard points out, Kipling may have professed to despise the aesthetes, but he "naturally share[d] much of the aesthetic or decadent structure of feeling" (1989, 49). He shared, above all, the perception that life is "no longer part of a predestined harmony but a partial struggle that has to be represented in a partial impressionistic way." One might notice, too, that Kipling's preoccupation with an imaginative transfiguration of the "ordinary," with the finding of beauty in what others see as fag ends, vulgarity, and detritus, has many analogues in late-nineteenth-century aesthetic theory and practice. Such concerns are found in contexts as diverse as Henley's *London Voluntaries* (1893) and Henry James's comment that the "most interesting experiments" of which art is capable "are hidden in the bosom of common things" (1962, 36).

Kipling stands at an odd angle to this later-nineteenth-century concern with the seemingly banal, shallow, and mediocre. Often self-conscious artistic engagement with third-rate material was making a bid for a tour de force. The Goncourts in *Renée Mauperin,* Flaubert in *Un Cœur Simple,* or George Moore in *Esther Waters* were displaying their art all the more effectively by employing it on dull or unpromising subjects. By contrast, Kipling, though as much a studious craftsman as they, celebrated a hidden but authentic beauty. The "Envoi" of *Life's Handicap* (1891) links the treatment of mundane subjects to the recovery of man's lost spiritual vision and stature. God,

> lest of all thought of Eden fade
> Bring'st Eden to the craftsman's brain

> Godlike to muse o'er his own trade
> And Manlike stand with God again.
>
> (Kipling 1892, 352)

To "see naught common on Thy Earth" and to encourage such perception in others is "to help such men as need." It is to mitigate some of the grief of life, the "horror of desolation, abandonment and realised worthlessness" of which Kipling was to speak to the young men at McGill. The remedy he was to offer in that speech was a simple, primary act of imaginative engagement in the daily life of others, to "interest yourself, to lose yourself—in some issue not personal to yourself—in another man's trouble, or, preferably, another man's joy." This means of escape from deceptive, subjective sensation is also a means by which one may accept that there was nothing irremediable, ineffaceable, or irrevocable in anything "said or thought or done" (1928, 20).

A belief in the imagination as a means to moral health or as a way of recapturing a lost vision of wholeness or harmony is, of course, part of the general heritage of romanticism. Kipling gives this heritage an idiosyncratic twist. The artist is inspired by a force outside himself and his own personality is insignificant. At the same time, in order not to betray this gift of inspiration, he must be a meticulous craftsman. The artist persona of "L'Envoi" is conceived in the image of one of the largely anonymous masons laboring to build a "dread temple" to God's "worth," believing that any success he may have is "compelled" by his Master, while his failure is his own.

Such expressions of Kipling's artistic purposes are easy to dismiss as relics of conventional piety. Such expressions certainly do not resonate with some currently fashionable critical approaches to, or discourse about, Kipling's work. However, "L'Envoi" and several other declarations like it open up another range of inquiry. How useful would it be to consider Kipling's texts as produced, to a substantial degree, from a direct, conscious relationship, through his own early pain ("I know of what I speak") to the pain and the visions of horror current in his time and culture? How central in Kipling's writing was the search for meaning, value, and significance that would heal that pain, or fend off that horror; a search pursued on the political, moral, and religious planes, through original and highly sophisticated explorations of history and of myth? Certainly such a view of Kipling is different from others currently on offer. Such views include the maimed and gifted obsessive concerned to cover his emotional tracks, the meticulous craftsman posing as a vocal philistine, the hurt child who converted imaginative yearning and joy into power "because desire is coded within a colonial system that sanctifies control and domination" (Sullivan 1993, 2). What is there to be said for a Kipling who knew and used his own suffering, searching for strategies to deal with the temptations of pessimism that he had known and that were also the prevailing temptations in a political and intellectual crisis he felt obliged to address?

There is at least some contemporary evidence for such a view, in the comments of those who did not share Kipling's politics and had little sympathy with imperialism. Mrs. Oliphant's remarks on *Life's Handicap* contain suggestions, which may be duplicated elsewhere, about the effect of Kipling's work on readers of the time:

> Those, however, who wish to avoid pain, must not go to Mr. Rudyard Kipling for pleasure. The thrill of emotion which he has the gift to send tingling through and through the reader is not of the easy kind. It is far from being the best of all possible worlds which he reveals to us; but it is something better. It is a world in which every cruel ill is confronted by that struggling humanity which is continually overborne, yet always victorious in defeat, in downfall and in death. (Green 1971, 136)

Such moralizing prose may seem dated and naive as literary discourse now. However, we may be too ready to dismiss as primitive what is not in this or last year's academic fashion. Mrs. Oliphant's and other comments like it do register an important point about Kipling's work. Apart from, or as well as, his professed imperialism, Kipling did appear to early readers to be concerned with fundamental questions of significance and meaning, moral, psychological, or "religious." Possibly some recent critics would deny the importance or even the existence of such questions considered as separate issues from those of "ideology," with which they are concerned. Kipling's ideology produced a false consciousness. He may have consciously pursued a quest for meaning but the only value such a quest has for the investigation lies in what it reveals of the exigencies and contradictions within imperialist discourse.

Such analysis as this is disabled by its own conceptual rigidity. John Ellis has shrewdly remarked on a weakness of the deconstructive terminology and mind-set Marxist and feminist critics sometimes borrow to the disadvantage of their own distinctive intellectual positions. In particular,

Ellis criticizes a habit of setting up an inflexible either-or as the only terms in which a subject can be discussed:

> All interpretation is abstraction. But abstraction can occur in a limitless number of ways which means that fundamentally different abstractions giving greater or lesser weight to different textual features do not differ from each other in one dimension but in any number; if one were to decide to focus on one particular abstraction (say a traditional one) and its opposite, one would have ruled out the search for all other kinds of abstractions. (1989, 81)

Even in a sophisticated form, such interpretative methodology, applied to Kipling's work, remains confined to a set of opposing terms:

> Kipling's packs and multiplicities transform and cross over some of the rigid binary constructions of nineteenth-century racist and gendered thought, entering in the process fluid and luminous borderline spaces. But it is precisely in those borderline sites that Kipling's anxieties over definition and structures become more exaggerated. His hedged and tightly framed narratives, then, expose, contain, limit, and defend themselves against the fearful yet seductive stories of Indian life, and in their ambivalence towards the embedded tales suggest some of the cracks in the ideological structures that sustained the dreams of empire. (Sullivan 1993, 8).

In spite of occasional expressions (such as "fluid and luminous borderline spaces") that suggest multiplicity or unexpected possibilities, the underlying frame of reference here is rigid. One is allowed no sense of the varieties of imperialism, the proliferating intricacy of its political, intellectual, and emotional crosscurrents, and the range of self-awareness in Kipling's own attitudes to imperialism and to the crisis of empire. Above all, one is given no notion of the complexity of the culture in which Kipling's texts were produced, a complexity implicit not only in those texts themselves but in the range and unexpectedness of the contemporary response they evoked.

What quality was it that in the words of Chesterton, a political opponent, made Kipling's work "a new breath of prophecy and promise" that filled "the age with a new change and stir, and gave to the pessimists something which if not a cure, was at least an antidote and a counter irritant?" (1950, 88).

Mrs. Oliphant's remark that "the thrill of emotion" Kipling sent tingling through his readers was not of an "easy kind" is perceptive. He did not underestimate the pain for which he offered a counterirritant. He presents, in all its frightfulness, and without facile consolation or rationalizing, the vision of horror and futility that overwhelms individuals as well as cities and kingdoms and powers. If there is a way of dealing with that vision, such a way exacts a high price.

Many critics have emphasized the effects of the Boer War and the First World War on Kipling's work. Obviously these events made Kipling more aware of the failings, moral and intellectual, of the British political elite. The wars brought home to him the fundamental insecurity and fragility that his own, hitherto lucky civilization shared with any other:

> Life so long untroubled, that ye who inherit forget
> It was not made with the mountains, it was not one with the deep.
> Men, not gods, devised it. Men not gods must keep.
>
> (Eliot 1973, 130)

Clearly, however, Kipling had a sense of the fundamental insecurity of life, will, sanity, and order from the outset of his career. Before and beneath his later concerns about military unpreparedness ("The Islanders"), about the ruling elite's incompetence, lack of foresight, and slavery to effete tradition ("Below the Mill Dam"), or the studies of various individual breakdowns lay a primal awareness of mysterious and unexpected danger in the very fact of living. From his beginnings as a writer he sensed a potential or actual horror at the heart of things. Intellect, will power, capacity to act, and even ability to make sense of the world were not given and unchanging facts. They were precariously maintained and sometimes lost to an outer or inner blackness, chaos, or destruction.

The "rather nasty story" that Kipling "with moderate good luck" (1971, 13) hoped to place in *Longman's Magazine* in 1887, and thus to inaugurate his literary career in London, provides useful evidence of his early concern with disintegration. Then and now challenging, and to some readers deeply offensive, "The Mark of the Beast" is a study of the breakdown of personality, of what is perceived as human nature, of the codes and values of Western European civilization. According to one account, Andrew Lang wrote that he would have given five pounds not to have read "this poisonous stuff" and William Sharpe, the critic and poet, prophesied its author would die mad before he was thirty. However one reads it, "The Mark of the Beast" is a threatening text (1971, 13–14).

It is also a text that lends itself very easily to recent interest in colonialist discourse and the relation of the "Other" to the codes of imperialism. Such readings would probably interpret the narrator's ironic stance as a distancing device to circumvent the violent and destructive eruption within the text. It is a strategy to evade knowledge that would threaten the values of the white elite. The horseplay and high spirits of the drunken officers and civil servants at the New Year's Eve party display the "homosocial bonding" and "masculinist ethic" that insecurely suppress the feminine and the "Other." Such suppression is, of course, only a part of the psychological damage imperialism brings about. Fleet's profanation of the monkey god Hanuman, while clearly revealing imperial arrogance and ignorance, may well also evoke fears of evolutionary reversion current in much late-nineteenth-century thought. The critic will see such fears as involving a yielding to unspoken, perhaps unspeakable, sexual desire; parallels to such texts as *The Picture of Dorian Gray* or *The Strange Case of Dr. Jekyll and Mr. Hyde* will be more or less plausibly evoked. The attentive reader will not fail to note the significant details of the appearance and behavior of the leper who punishes Fleete's sacrilege. "Perfectly naked," with a body that "shone like frosted silver"(Kipling 1892, 210), he cries like the mewing of an otter" (211) and "drops his head on Fleete's breast before we could wrench him away." This cannot be mistaken for anything but an eruption of the repressed homosexuality that threatens to destabilize the homosocial, masculinized imperialist ethos. The recognition of this explains the narrator's and Strickland's sadistic violence. The tortures they inflict on the leper to force him to lift the curse are attempts to restore the sexual stereotyping on which the imperial ideology is predicated. Enacting these tortures, the two men themselves receive the "mark of the beast." Their code has been permanently fractured and subverted.

Such readings appeal to some contemporary political and historical predilections and to certain varieties of gender theory. Interpretations along these lines are far from being obviously groundless. Granted an initial sympathy with the political and historical premises on which they are based, such readings may be presented in a fairly plausible way and supported by at least a selection of details from the text. The problem lies in the narrow field of preoccupations to which such intellectual premises confine the reader and in the questionable nature of the premises themselves.

A less doctrinaire political and ideological context might offer the possibility of a more profitable line of inquiry into "The Mark of the Beast." It might be more useful to consider the mythic and "religious" implications of this early excursion into horror and chaos. Reading the text as what, at least prima facie, it appears to be—a highly wrought, highly self-conscious rendering of the danger inherent in ruling alien cultures—might offer a view more inclusive of its various aspects. The "native proverb" that stands as the epigraph to the tale ("Your Gods and my Gods—do you or I know which are the stronger?") touches on questions raised and settled, at least nominally, for Western Europeans in ancient religious history. It was the issue between Elijah and the prophets of Baal. (For a historical and cultural tradition that still in its textbook versions professed to rest on Israel as well as Greece and Rome, such narratives remained central.) The question of the power of the God is the question of his ability to protect his people. The doubt, if not the Old Testament phraseology, was widespread in the culture of the time. It is implied in *Lord Jim*, in the description of Jim's father's religious certitude, the "certain knowledge of the unknown" he enjoyed in a rectory that "glowed with a warm tint" (Conrad 1989, 5), or in the beautiful illusions entertained by Kurtz's fiancée about her betrothed's mission and ideals in "The Heart of Darkness." Neither the knowledge of one nor the illusions of the other have meaning and potency in places where "the direct sway of providence ceases."

The view that "The Mark of the Beast" "ironizes, deflates and subverts the position" the narrator and "Strickland have fought so hard to sustain" (Sullivan 1993, 10)—their role as Englishmen—is too simple. The ironies of the text make it far more fluid and teasing than such an account suggests. Irony colors the initial statement that "east of Suez . . . Man" is "handed over to the power of the Gods and Devils of Asia" (Kipling 1892, 208). Yet this is only what "some hold," a "theory" that "may be stretched to explain my story." The word "stretched" is significant. Doubts about the validity of Western civilization or about the power of the Christian God in alien territories offer a ready and plausible interpretation of the particular facts to be recounted. However, such an interpretation may not necessarily be a true one. The phrase "unnecessary horrors of life in India" is worth a moment's pause. "Unnecessary" suggests that what follows is not simply natural, unavoidable, or inevitable. It is not a question of an intolerable climate, the power of an alien culture or "alien gods" (however that phrase is interpreted). It is not the usual problem of ruling over or negotiating with other races or the dilemmas inherent in any exercise of power at all. Rather it is something that need not have happened. The reference to the doctor Dumoise who had already appeared in "By Word of Mouth" begins to throw a little more light on these "unnecessary horrors." The "curious manner" of Dumoise's death "elsewhere described" is juxtaposed with the doctor's failure to understand the Mark of the Beast. It will be remembered from the earlier tale that Dumoise and his wife were "two little people" (1907, 315) who "retired from the world after their marriage." The wife's death from typhoid was the result of the couples' creation of their own isolated, enclosed life. "Dumoise was wrong in shutting himself from the world for a year" (319) since, when his wife "went down," he was too shy to ask for the help others were ready to give. Far simpler than "The Mark of the Beast," "By Word of Mouth" effectively contrasts the isolated life the "Dormice" tried to live with the Indian world where the supernatural is readily accepted and the "bounds of the Possible" (318) are drawn far differently. Dumoise, "the best of good fellows though dull" (319), cannot himself reach the dead wife he adores. However, he can hear from her "by word of mouth" through his idle and dishonest servant, in a culture where the possibility of such communication is not suppressed or denied.

The early mention of Dumoise in "The Mark of the Beast" has several connotations. There is the obvious irony that the little doctor who denies the supernatural significance of Fleete's collapse is himself to die "in a rather curious manner" (208) after a message from his dead wife. More than this, the reference to the earlier tale confirms the theme of willful cultural isolation and chosen ignorance, of the attempt to maintain one's own codes or way of life, cut off from the wider world of India. Fleete is not "imperialism" in the abstract. He is a very specific social type within British India. Devoid of function or a sense of social duty, having neither work nor role in the Raj, he merely "owned" (1892, 208) some land left him by an uncle and has come out to "finance" it. The comment "of course" in the statement "His knowledge of natives was, of course, limited" is an invitation to locate Fleete as a familiar type, faintly irritating to old India hands. This comment also modifies the earlier remark that Strickland knew "as much of natives of India as is good for any man" (208). The way to be safe and effective in contracts with an alien culture lies between the extremes of too much and too little knowledge. The ignorant are in special danger if they lie outside the nexus of labor, rule, and responsibility, if their contract with the subject land is merely financial.

The account of the horseplay at the club New Year party underlines the difference between Fleete's drunkenness and that of the local officers and administrators. For the latter, the night is "excusably wet," a well-earned relaxation. Men who guard the frontiers of empire, continually "at the risk of a Khyberee bullet" (209), have "a right to be riotous." The schoolboy romping and antics are shown as an escape from the ever-present risk of death faced by those who, as they fool about, are "taking stock of [their] losses in dead or disabled that had fallen during the past year" (209). The text briefly refers to victories and defeats, the annexation of Burma, and the clash with the Sudanese tribesmen at Suakim. (These were the warriors who "broke a British square" in Kipling's poem "Fuzzy-Wuzzy.") Those at the club party who have not been engaged in such fighting have been trying "to make money on insufficient experiences" (209). This resumé of the mixed fortunes and doubtful finances of empire in the 1880s economically establishes a context for Kipling's narrator. It is also a perception of the variety of imperial relationships and conduct that some recent criticism with its rigid categories ("colonialism," "the Other," etc.) fails to recognize. The Raj contains Fleete and these young officers and civil servants. Fleete's ungentlemanly anger at his horse, his mistreatment of the animal, and the "Guard of Dishonour" (210) formed to take him home after his binge all confirm him as a rank outsider, however "genial, and inoffensive" (208) he may be.

The significance of Fleete's profaning of the image of the image of Hanuman, "a leading divinity worthy of respect" (210), is clearly crucial to the meaning of "The Mark of the Beast." Before speculating on analogies with Dorian Gray or Jekyll and Hyde, on the growing awareness of multiple facets to the personality or on (notional) sexual fears and repression of the period, it is worth considering the figure of Hanuman himself. He was the ally of the righteous paragon Rama in the epic struggles of *The Ramayana*. The monkey discovered the prince's kidnapped wife in Ceylon and took part in the final battles with the tyrant Ravan. Hanuman's courage, kindness, and loyalty won him the reward of immortality. His story embodies a spiritual progress and an ascent from a lower to a higher form of life.

Fleete's grinding the ashes of his cigar butt into the forehead of the stone image is more than a casual insult. He is denying, or refusing to know, the spiritual content of Hinduism, the inner meaning of what, to him, is simply a grotesque idol. Complaining of "the difficulties of the language" (208), he knows nothing of the culture he degrades and "solemnly" claims responsibility for the mark. ("I made it" [210].) Appropriately, his punishment is a reversal of the spiritual progress Hanuman represents. Repetitions (the "Silver Man" whose "body shone like frosted silver" [210]) give a faintly ritualist air to the leper's sudden appearance "without any warning." The biblical phrase "a leper white as snow" confirms the uncanny religious significance of the Silver Man. The words recall the punishment of Elisha's servant Gehazi (2 Kings 6:30) for sacrilege and corruption. (Kipling was to use the expression years later in this sense in a notable political poem attacking Rufus Isaacs.) The leper "is not one of the regular priests of the temple" (215). The narrative enhances the effect of dread by leaving his exact identity and origins obscure. However, the text hints at black magic ("I understood how men and women and little children can endure to see a witch burnt alive"). "Can" rather than "could" is a crucial and interesting variant from the expected tense. "Can" suggests that this spiritual evil is not some seventeenth-century fantasy but a living possibility. Clearly, the wider collapse of personality and of human nature the magic brings about includes a loss of sexual identity. In fact, the text is so explicit about the sexual aspect of Fleete's disintegration that it is difficult to see repressed sexuality as, in itself, an explanation of what is happening or as an irruption of "unspeakable" material that fractures the brittle rhetoric of imperialism. Instead, sexuality is simply one feature, among others, of a "giving way" (217) of the human spirit. The horrible love call of the leper, "something without mewing like a she-otter" (218), is given the same weight as Fleete's growing appetite for half-raw chops, "bloody ones with gristle" (216).

"The Mark of the Beast" is a study of the breakdown of law, of the fragility of civilization and restraint and of the horror lying outside the circle of order, a horror that, at best, that circle barely keeps back. Two causes are offered for the breakdown. First, the ruling elite have thrown up such a specimen as Fleete, willfully ignorant, functionless, and merely parasitic. Second, the victims of his insolence have refused recourse to the law that is available to them. "There was a section of the Indian Penal Code which exactly met Fleete's offence" (212). Fleete's crime might have been punished within the system, whatever the faults of that system may have been.

The descent of the narrator and Strickland into gleefully sadistic torturers trying to force the leper to lift his curse and reverse Fleete's disintegration is an instance of what waits when the covenant, or tour de force of civilization, is rejected. It is followed by an uneasy, embarrassed resuming of roles, an attempt to pretend that nothing has happened. Obviously Fleete, Strickland, and the narrator have disgraced themselves "as Englishmen for ever" (223). Arguably, the narrator's view of himself has been permanently changed. Yet the priests of Hanuman are as anxious as the English to paper over the incident and what it has revealed. When Strickland tried to "offer redress for the pollution of the god" he was "solemnly assured that no white man had ever touched the idol, and that he was an incarnation of all the virtues labouring under a delusion" (223).

The object of this book is to explore various aspects of the preoccupations revealed by such a reading of "The Mark of the Beast." It offers a line of inquiry different from current interests in the hidden, unnameable, and disruptive, in the threatened unity of texts and various unsuccessful strategies of evasion. Instead, this study adopts the premise that Kipling's texts embody, and are often driven by, a highly sophisticated awareness of the problems of maintaining, and of giving some kind of legitimacy to, rule and order and of the darkness and horror that wait if those problems are not solved.

This book begins by examining *Puck of Pook's Hill* and *Rewards and Fairies,* still somewhat neglected items in the Kipling canon. Nominally children's stories, they offer some of Kipling's most subtle meditations on myth and history and some of his most interesting articulations of the dilemmas of rule and order. The next chapters deal with attempts to meet the encompassing darkness or to mitigate its destructive effects by various kinds of restoration or reintegration. These chapters focus on the important pre–First World War story "The House Surgeon" and the postwar collection *Limits and Renewals.* Next, an exploration of the late story "The Eye of Allah" considers Kipling's treatment the theme of the knowledge a culture finds unbearable. The book concludes with a reading of the little-known "Proofs of Holy Writ," one of Kipling's relatively few explicit handlings of the themes of art in general, of his own art in particular, and of how it might help such men as need.

1
Failure and Success of Civilizations in *Puck of Pook's Hill*

The structure of *Puck of Pook's Hill*, and the analogies between its two main plots, Norman and Roman, are among the perennially interesting topics in Kipling criticism. As J. M. S. Tompkins long ago suggested (1965, 77–78), Kipling does not intend, nor should the reader assume, positive and limited modern parallels for his historical re-creations, as, for instance, that Hadrian's Wall "means" the northwest frontier of British India and the Winged Hats the Russians. Hardly anyone would deny that this is to impoverish the stories, to rob them of their curious power as myth.

That power is the first fact about them. An incomparable vividness of realization in the physical details, the sheer presence of characters like De Aquila and Maximus, is combined with a resonance in the stories, a feeling that they contain some deep underlying meaning. It is a mystery that a schematized, overly simple reading easily destroys. One can sympathize with Angus Wilson's suggestion that *Puck of Pook's Hill* is best viewed as a series of striking incidents in the relationship of barbarism and civilization, order and disorder. He seems unwilling to go beyond the commonly accepted opinion that the arrangement of the tales (the placing of the rise of Norman England *before* the twilight of Roman Britain) endorses the hopeful message that order will rise again out of chaos. There is also, he concedes, some general sense of a *cyclical* view of history, an interest in a parallel between Imperial Rome and the Edwardian British Empire. Wilson seems to feel that to go further, as other critics have tried to do, into the intellectual structure of *Puck of Pook's Hill* is to diminish it. Its imaginative quality is primitive and mythic, a given fact rather than an intellectual construction.

Despite this sensitive critic's misgivings, the reader probably cannot refrain from seeing connections in the two cycles of stories. They relate to each other in the broad outlines of their themes and in many of their details. Hints broken off in one section are taken up and more fully developed in the other. Even if we cannot be sure we have grasped it, the full meaning of *Puck of Pook's Hill* does seem to lie in its totality. It is too much of a unity to read as a series of heightened, unrelated moments.

Some lines of investigation may be found in the conflicting "historicisms" of the late nineteenth century. Kipling would have gained more than historical facts from the careful reading in the Cape Town Library, undertaken as a preliminary to *Puck of Pook's Hill*. He would have moved in a world of historical interpretation now defunct, and hard imaginatively to reconstruct. The racial framework of much of this historical theorizing was, of course, discredited after the 1930s. It now seems alien, often naive, and, to many, repulsive. It is possible, with hindsight, to discover sinister undercurrents in what, at the time, appeared respectable scholarship.

But apart from the dubious validity of such an exercise, it prevents investigation of Kipling's relationship to the historical interpretation of his time—the question of what he made imaginatively from something many readers would now see as a highly dubious body of thought. The dismissal of that tradition is so complete that it becomes impossible to see that it might be used, by an artist, in ways more or less intelligent and humane. What emerges from *Puck of Pook's Hill* is very much to Kipling's credit. He makes the best possible use, and a highly sophisticated one at that, of the universe of historical discourse in which he and his contemporaries moved.

As well as the interest Wilson mentions in a parallel between Imperial Rome and Imperial Britain, one of the principal features of historiography was, without doubt, the conflict between the largely racial interpretations of the fall of the Roman Empire. Writers like E. A. Freeman, or the immensely successful popularizer J. R. Green, made a case that the Germanic immigration into the moribund world of the fifth century revitalized it. They presented a picture, drawn perhaps ultimately from Tacitus's *Germania* and mediated through contemporary German historians such as Treitschke, of the contrast between the virile and healthy Teutons and the degenerate Latin races. One of their strongest arguments seems to have been the notion that, while the Roman heritage in its late phase was despotic and bureaucratic, the Germans or Scandinavians had free institutions. It was from the *Thing* that the idea of Parliament allegedly emerged.

1 / Civilizations in *Puck of Pook's Hill* 39

The "Teutonic Theory" was of course hotly contested, though still within racial assumptions. The husband of Kipling's cousin Margaret, the great Latin scholar J. W. Mackail, staunch defender of the use of the classics in secondary schools, saw the fall of Rome as the result of racial adulteration, and the Germanic peoples as inferior stock. In a lecture as late as 1928 he described the *Volkerwanderung* as

> a steadily increasing infiltration of less civilised populations into the area of a higher civilisation which was not potent enough to absorb them. . . . The result was that the level of European civilisation became permanently lowered. The old culture perished. It is the same danger which the United States and more than one of our own dominions, have in recent years realised and taken pains to check by stringent restrictions on immigration. (1929, 26–27)

Much earlier, in his well-known textbook *Latin Literature*, he had vigorously asserted the classical heritage. Civilization was the creation, almost solely, of Rome:

> So long as mankind will look before and after, the name of Rome will be the greatest of those upon which their backward glance can be turned. . . . Law, government, citizenship are all the creation of the Latin Race. (1934, 385)

Mackail's view suggests how pervasive racial interpretations were when Kipling was gathering his materials for *Puck of Pook's Hill*. Such opinions were found right across the political spectrum. Mackail, "Little Englander," admirer of William Morris, supporter of the Independent Labour Party, was far to the left of Kipling. In consequence, though quite friendly, they were never close. Yet Mackail accepted, as did his contemporaries, ideas that would be found now, if anywhere, only in discreditable circles of the extreme Right—an illustration of the danger of reading the past with the presumptions of the present.

Nominally a children's storybook, *Puck of Pook's Hill* gives a subtle reinterpretation of the forgotten controversy between "Teutonic Theory" and "Classical Heritage." An important element in the book is lost if it is regarded as offering a merely cyclical interpretation of history. Juxtaposition of Norman and Roman is juxtaposition of success with failure. More seems implied by the relationship between the two sets of stories than the guarded optimism Wilson allows—that order will return in time. Kipling does appear, in his account of the rise of England and the fall of Rome, to suggest *reasons* for these events.

Something is lacking in the failure that accounts for the success. One civilization, despite acts of heroism that temporarily stave off disintegration, is declining. The other is moving forward and developing. The two cycles of stories focus on the causes of these processes. They are far from simple. Kipling operates by hints and inferences. But enough is intimated to indicate a far more complex and intelligent reading of historical change than either the upholders of the "Teutonic Theory" or their Classical opponents provided.

The parallels between the two cycles, the elements they have in common, are their most immediately noticeable features. Both involve the virtues of comradeship and the guarding of a threatened gateway from attack (Pevensey and Hadrian's Wall). In each cycle there is a journey among the barbarians for negotiation or renewal—Parnesius among the Picts and "The Joyous Venture." In each case a civilization is shown in its relations with those outside its boundaries, geographical or cultural. In each case, too, the defenders of the frontier are shown in relation to the central authority. Both cycles offer a picture of the leader and the spell he casts. The thematic, and to some extent structural, kinship between the two sets of stories seems inescapable. The meaning Kipling attaches to the parallels is less clear.

A convenient starting point might well be Weland, smith to the Norse gods. Kipling, perhaps misled by one of his sources (see Green 1965, 204) or perhaps deliberately, assumes that Weland was once much more important in Scandinavian religion than the few remaining references to him suggest. In any case, Weland is chosen by Kipling to explore certain elements of the historical myth he wishes to develop. Some of these are mentioned by Wilson: the arrival of gods, cultures, and religions and their gradual acclimatization, dilution, and disappearance. Kipling offers a first stark picture of Weland, the great black image in the bows of a Viking pirate ship, with icicles on its lips: "When he saw me he began a long chant in his own tongue, telling me how he was going to rule England, and how I should smell the smoke of his altars from Lincolnshire to the Isle of Wight" (Kipling 1930, 17).

He then moves from this initial glimpse of a horrifying power to a quaint picture of the demoted god plying his trade around the countryside, as Puck had prophesied. The result of this double vision of Weland is subtle. The numen of the god is rendered harmless, the human sacrifices becoming tokens before being abandoned altogether. But a hint of the mystery remains. The English culture, whose growth Kipling is to sketch, is rooted in something dark, powerful, not entirely explicable. When Weland departs he must be correctly "paid," granted formal valediction and release. Some of his power remains in his sword with its runic inscription.

The meaning of Kipling's mythic opening, like the significance of the legends and folklore whose power it imitates, is hard to define. Among other nuances, it suggests the connection and dependence of the rational order and civilization on the powers, the mysteries of the nonrational "barbarism." Significantly, it is Weland's sword and the runes upon it that save the lives of the Knights of the Joyous Venture when they fall into Witta's hands. It bridges barbarism and civilization, making a connection that Parnesius, despite great and intelligent effort, fails to make.

The link of a culture with its primitive, half-legendary roots is asserted as a fact of vital importance, though hedged about with safeguards. Kipling is far from dallying with irrationalism or wishing to revive "dark forces," as D. H. Lawrence, for example, did in *The Plumed Serpent*. Weland has really gone, having declined from dark force to crotchety old man. A delicate balance is struck between this and the contrasting fact of the surviving magic of his sword.

The runic inscription on that sword, as Kipling gives it, is a prophecy of the future emergence of national institutions, freedom and law, and of their intimate connection with, and unfolding from, something dark, barbaric, numinous:

> *The Gold I gather*
>
> *Comes in to England,*
> *Out of deep Water.*
>
> *Like a shining Fish*
> *Then it descends*
> *Into deep Water.*
> *It is not given*
> *For goods or gear.*
> *But for The Thing.*

(135–36)

The *Thing* (Parliament, that is) is prophesied in terms that makes its emergence seem holy and magical, not just a sensible constitutional arrangement. The author of the much later *Pageant of Parliament* has provided in

Puck of Pook's Hill not an account of the political history of an institution or a concept, freedom under law, but of their hidden side. He offers a picture of their emergence out of the yearnings, deeds, and renunciations of individuals who do not know each other. Concept and institution grow from what is almost a kind of collective unconscious. Weland personifies the most purely magical element in this process. The tendency of myth to connect human institutions, states, or ruling families with the gods or the supernatural is a tendency so common throughout history, and so satisfying, as simply to be a fact of human nature. The tone of the description of Weland handing on the sword, mildly humorous but retaining a sense of power, is a high example of literary tact. It is mystery without mystification and awe without obscurantism.

It is also, incidentally, a concession to the "Teutonic Theory." Free institutions were, it appears, ultimately of Germanic origin, and Parliament was, like the English royal family, "Woden-Born." It is with a calculated shock that, long after the disappearance of Weland, the sword's power should reappear, the meaning of the runes still deliberately concealed:

> He [Witta] spoiled us of all we had, but when he laid hands on Hugh's sword and saw the runes on the blade hastily he thrust it back. Yet his covetousness overcame him and he tried again and again, and the third time the Sword sang loud and angrily, so that the rowers leaned on their oars to listen. (74–75)

Of course, this is only one element in the story Kipling tells. The mystery is to be modified by other factors. But this is the vital clue. Civilized man and barbarian are linked in a shared awareness of the unknown and holy.

The Roman cycle in *Puck of Pook's Hill* provides many rational and commonsense causes for the decline of the Roman polity, such as the "splitting of the eagles" or division of the empire, or the deterioration of leadership in such figures as Parnesius's commander on the Wall. Beyond these, however, lies something else—the failure of the "myth," the disappearance of the wellspring of nonrational power from a political institution.

Kipling deliberately makes it easy to overlook Parnesius's attitude to his father's notion that Rome is lost because it forsook its gods: "He went back to the time of Diocletian; and to listen to him you would have thought Eternal Rome herself was on the edge of destruction, just because a few people had become a little large minded" (153). It is a hint that might be

1 / Civilizations in *Puck of Pook's Hill* 43

overlooked as the remark of a mere reactionary, as in part no doubt it is. Yet here perhaps is the clue. Parnesius himself has a religion about which the reader is left in no doubt, the solders' faith in Mithras, god of light, victorious over darkness.

There seems little reason to doubt Kipling's sympathy with what he knew or assumed about Mithraism. In his last collection, *Limits and Renewals,* there are many suggestions that he saw it as similar in spirit to Freemasonry, as a religion of male comradeship and the pursuit of "enlightenment," tolerant ("Many roads Thou hast fashioned: all of them lead to the Light!"), and strong in the loyalty of an elite group. However, what is impressive is his awareness of what it did not satisfy. He was to deal with this in *Limits and Renewals* in two stories of the clash of St. Paul with the ethos of the ancient world: "The Church that was at Antioch" and "The Manner of Men."

In *Puck of Pook's Hill* the awareness is already present, in a subtle and deeply eloquent moment. Parnesius turns aside to offer his prayer to the setting sun, "deep, splendid-sounding words" that we do not hear (though we have "A Song to Mithras" later as testimony to what they must have been). Instead, at this point, Puck leads the children away, chanting something that is no longer classical Latin:

> *Cur mundus militat sub vana gloria*
> *Cujus prosperitas est transitoria?*
> *Tam cito labitur ejus potentia*
> *Quam vasa figuli quae sunt fragilia.*
> *Quo Caesar abiit celsus imperio?*
> *Vel Dives splendidus totus in prandio?* . . .
>
> (162)

These lines are in fact from a thirteenth-century poem of doubtful authorship, but they resemble the early hymns of the Dark Ages, such as those of Prudentius or Venantius Fortunatus. The sentiments look forward to monastic Christianity. Dives and Caesar are equated. All worldly power is as fragile as a jar from the potter's wheel. Underemphasized as this moment is, its meaning can be seen. This is the force that will triumph, not Mithraism.

Although Christianity had been the official religion of the empire for fifty years by the presumed date of the Roman cycle, Kipling does not allow Parnesius to mention its existence. The oddity of this has struck more than one commentator. It appears to be a deliberate device, in conjunction with Puck's overriding of Parnesius's Mithraism with a "Christian hymn." Parnesius's military values are about to be overwhelmed, yet he does not really suspect it, attaching no importance to, refusing to see, the force accomplishing the change:

> *Shadow to shadow, well persuaded, saith,*
> *"See how our works endure!"*

(139)

The renunciation of the world, already beginning in the West in the supposed period of Parnesius, answers a general feeling of the time, expressed in Puck's hymn, and has the power to create a new civilization. For an added poignance, Kipling follows the hymn with "A British-Roman Song" ("My father's father saw it not . . ." [163]), the provincial's appeal to the eternity of the empire, and unavailing request to the city to guard the imperial fire.

The civic virtue, the esprit de corps of the Mithraist soldiery, has not the same power of extension beyond itself to the barbarian or the alien as the sword in the Norman cycle. Amal, a fellow-Mithraist, is spared by Parnesius, but they fight on. Yet the Knights of the Joyous Venture go on their vitally important journey with Witta, cooperate with him in winning the gold, and part on the warmest of terms. Parnesius and Pertinax can *negotiate* with the Picts, winning time, making rational attempts to understand them, but in their journeys beyond the Wall they cannot reach them at a deeper level. They have no magic, or numen, with which to bind civilized man and barbarian. Kipling already, in an unforgettable landscape of "altars to Legions and Generals forgotten, and broken statues of Gods and Heroes" (170) and in the bricked-up entrance to the "Province of Valentia," has suggested what "A Pict Song" goes on to confirm: that Roman civilization is imposed from above and maintained by force alone. "A Pict Song" voices, in different words, the complaint of Tacitus's barbarian chieftain: "They make a wilderness and call it Peace."

The Picts, "the worm in the wood," "Moths making holes in a cloak" (225), the conquered but irreconcilable weak, are not attractive. Timid, treacherous resentment seldom is. Nevertheless, they are understandable, and Kipling has done them imaginative justice. They are a permanent problem to the imperial system that bears down on them; one that, constituted as it is, it cannot solve.

1 / Civilizations in *Puck of Pook's Hill* 45

Puck of Pook's Hill's underlying theme is this very problem of the creation of a lasting polity through reconciling the weak, defeated, and alien to its institutions. Part of the solution appears to be to retain the power of the nonrational—the mana, the runes on Weland's sword. Other aspects are easier to apprehend and state rationally. The friendship of Norman and Saxon—Young Men at the Manor, and their bond later with the Viking Witta—is radically different from Parnesius's patronizing relationship with Allo or his attitude to Amal, an enemy one respects. Barriers are really crossed in the Norman cycle that remain in the Roman. (The dominant feature of the first is Pevensey, a gate; of the second, Hadrian's Wall, a barrier.) There is the curious all-embracing companionship of the Joyous Venture, including even a captured Chinese, and the courtesy and understanding in the winning of the Lady Aelueva both exemplify humanity and the breaking of barriers. But it is the last story in the collection that enforces the meaning of the whole.

"The Treasure and the Law" shows that Kipling wears his "Teutonic Theory" with a difference. The *Thing* may have its dim beginning with Weland, but it is when the barons' embryonic "Parliament" at Runnymede promises equality and justice to the persecuted outsider, the Jew Kadmiel, that final reconciliation can be achieved. His secret action in throwing the gold into the sea is the act of adherence of the alien and weak, which means that this polity, unlike the Roman, will survive and has the power of growth.

Kadmiel is an extraordinarily vivid embodiment of the problem already suggested in the Picts who work to bring down Rome. It is the problem incidentally touched on by Nietzsche in his concept of ressentiment, resentment by the weak of the power of the strong. Kipling and Nietzsche are at one in recognizing the importance of the phenomenon. No rule or civilization can be safe that does not take account of the irreconciled weak and the urge to exercise power, which they are compelled to suppress. Kipling and Nietzsche diverge fundamentally on the question of a solution.

Where Nietzsche simply urges the strong to repudiate the weak, Kipling focuses *Puck of Pook's Hill* on inclusion and healing. He suggests that Kadmiel is forced to lead two lives, to conceal his inner existence: "He twitched his gown over his shoulders, and a square plate of gold, studded with jewels, gleamed for an instant through the fur, like a star through flying snow" (291).

The text stresses the contrast between his two voices, one deep and thunderous, the other "thin and waily" (286), between his concealed wealth and knowledge and his outward vulnerability. His response to oppression has been, like the Picts, to seek power through subterfuge: "We sought Power—Power—Power! That is our God in our captivity. Power to use!" (293).

Kipling, by the parallel with the Picts, implies that this urge is far from confined to the Jews. It is simply the reverse side, the almost inevitable concomitant, of all "Cities and Thrones and Powers," all dominion of the strong over the weak. The difference surpassing all the others, between the Roman Empire and the Norman tradition, is that in the latter an answer to this suppressed undercurrent has been found. Kadmiel's descendants are accepted members of the community, part of the English scene, rather than a submerged group: "They could see young Mr. Meyer, in his new yellow gaiters, very busy and excited at the end of the line and they could hear the thud of the falling birds" (302).

2
Rewards and Fairies:
Thor and Tyr, Necessary Suffering, and the Battle against Disorder

Rewards and Fairies has not received its fair share of close examination. Nor has it been valued as the complex and subtle work of art it is. It is thirty years since Roger Lancelyn Green commented on the book and its companion, *Puck of Pook's Hill,* saying "they are still often dismissed as merely for children" (1965, 11). Yet this remark remains substantially true. There is a curious paradox about the critical reputation of both works. They are praised and neglected. Eminent historians, such as G. M. Trevelyan, have celebrated their capacity to make the past physically present (quoted by Green 1965, 212). Literary critics readily and frequently admit this "impression of authenticity," in J. I. M Stewart's phrase (1966, 122), or the power the tales have to convey "the continuous flow of physical existence," as J. M. S. Tompkins puts it (1965, 75). The fairly limited body of critical writing on the stories, of which Tompkins's comments on Kipling's choice of "period" language remain among the most interesting (75), has concentrated on this quality, almost to the exclusion of others.

Critics show, besides, an unwillingness to take *Rewards and Fairies* quite seriously as art, to explore the pattern of theme and imagery within it. Philip Mason, for example, offers a sensitive account of "Cold Iron," stressing the importance of the theme of sacrifice in this story. He accepts that it has "different levels" (1975, 174) and that it is near the center of Kipling's thought (174). Nevertheless, he asserts, it is wrong to interpret it "on too intellectual a plane," since Kipling felt rather than thought what he wanted to say (175). Shamsul Islam's study *Kipling's Law* issues a similar caveat. Islam touches on the themes of law and sacrifice in "the Puck books" but remarks that the author's treatment of them is not "very consistent" (1975,

142), since he is mainly concerned to nourish the imagination of his childish audience.

Perhaps Philip Mason has pointed to the key problem about the meaning of *Rewards and Fairies:* the apparent inconsistency of its symbolism. How and in what way, he asks, can "cold iron," the binding image of the collection, be at once the symbol of redemptive suffering, of the power of the sword, and of custom and drudgery? As he says, these are "odd bedfellows" (Mason 1975, 178). His solution—that the link between them is the compulsion exercised by a man's own sense of duty and that in any case "cold iron" is an elastic symbol (177)—does not seem a satisfactory one.

It is likely that an answer to the problem of "inconsistency" that has perplexed scholars like Mason may be found in a closer look at the way in which Kipling uses Norse myth in the collection. This chapter will examine the first five stories in *Rewards and Fairies,* exploring how Kipling handles three main topics within them: the theme of sacrifice (the Thor/Tyr motif); the theme of maturation, or necessary suffering; and the order/disorder axis. Concentrating on the first five stories in the book seems sensible, given the way *Rewards and Fairies* is planned. I would suggest that the first five stories form a discrete unit. A second unit is formed by the two stories dealing with Pharaoh Lee: "Brother Square Toes" and "A Priest in Spite of Himself." These two tales handle the specific problem of how a worthy object of loyalty is to be discovered and propose an answer in the evolving consciousness of the originally rootless Gypsy and smuggler. Lee's response to the qualities of the Moravians and the Seneca Indians in his new American home influences him in the choice of the moral life. The two Pharaoh Lee stories form a coherent narrative that, although clearly linked to the wider themes of the book, may be best considered in its own terms. The last story in *Rewards and Fairies,* "The Tree of Justice," stands somewhat outside the moral scheme proposed in the collection. It offers a plea for mercy in its insistence that no many has any right to judge the oath-breaking King Harold who has refused the duty and sacrifice elsewhere insisted on. "The Tree of Justice" may, and in fact should, be considered separately. The other tales omitted from consideration—"The Conversion of St. Wilfrid," "A Doctor of Medicine," and "Simple Simon"—form another unit, a deliberate lightening of tone between the two serious cycles they follow and the disturbing story with which Kipling ends his work.

The myths of Thor and Tyr offered Kipling a framework within which he was able to bind together into a coherent whole moral perceptions that might otherwise have been unrelated. Of course, the myths of Thor and Tyr are as boldly refracted through the medium of Kipling's mind and art and bent as much to his purposes in *Rewards and Fairies* as the strikingly different Scandinavian fable of Weland had been in *Puck of Pook's Hill*. Weland and his sword, in the earlier book, had been used to suggest the dependence of civilization on barbarism, of the rational order on the powers and mysteries of the nonrational. The fable had provided the hidden side, as opposed to the public political history, of the concept of freedom under the law, and its emergence from the yearnings, deeds, and renunciations of individuals who do not know each other, yet who form almost a kind of collective unconscious.

Kipling deliberately and very markedly changes the key in the second collection. Puck in the crucial opening story "Cold Iron" is asked if the smith who made the slave-ring, the symbol of man's condition of service and servitude, was "Wayland." He replies that it was not. He would have passed the time of day with "Wayland Smith": "This other was different" (Kipling 1910, 12). As Thor is darker and more powerful than Weland, so the material mediated through myth in *Rewards and Fairies* is darker, more powerful, and not to be accommodated into the story of a developing civilization.

Scandinavian legends are explicitly referred to in several stories in *Rewards and Fairies,* most importantly in "Cold Iron" and in "The Knife and the Naked Chalk," which establish the book's moral frame of reference. However, the outlines of Norse mythology extend beyond particular references to Thor and Tyr, beyond even the recalling, in other stories, of those gods through objects related to them—the great trees (Davidson 1964, 86), the hammer, the neck-ring, cold iron. There is a close relationship between certain moral connotations of the Thor and Tyr legends and the entire complex of psychological intimations offered in *Rewards and Fairies*. It is difficult to define all these exactly, but among the most important is that of necessary suffering, the ordeal or *rite de passage* from child to adult. A related subject is the nature of a sacrifice, whether literally through death, a physical pain or, metaphorically, a surrender of the personality, which is the price paid to establish order, law, or civilization.

The stories also deal in varying degrees with the topic of duty. They show the difficulties of remaining faithful, the tests and strain of keeping one's bond. The substitution of Thor and Tyr for Weland is the entry to a darker region of the mind, where the matter in hand is not the building of a polity but something more painful: the binding of the Fenrir Wolf, the blunting of the appetite for chaos and darkness.

"Cold Iron," the gateway to the book's arduous moral journey, represents the leaving behind the chamber of maiden thought. On one level, it is a studious and significant reversal of the fairy story of Robin Goodfellow, the naughty boy who would not accept the adults' rules and was taken up by the fairies, who gave him the gifts of invisibility and the power to change his shape. Kipling takes this old legend of wish fulfillment, with its fantasy of escape into moral irresponsibility, and turns it inside out. The slave woman's child is offered the freedom of fantasy by Sir Huon and Lady Esclairmonde but chooses the humdrum condition of servitude.

On another level, the opening tale corresponds to the stage, described by mythographers like Mircea Eliade as *illo tempore,* the time when Earth and Heaven were close together, when communication between the realms of natural and supernatural was relatively easy (Eliade 1972, 58). The breakup of this closeness and the emergence of the much harder human condition we know is a constant eschatological theme of myth and folktale. Kipling's variant of it connects the reversal of the Robin Goodfellow theme to a law of life. The child *chooses* servitude to Cold Iron knowingly: "It goes with Flesh and Blood, and one can't prevent it" (Kipling 1910, 8). The legend of the metal that keeps the fairies at bay is broadened and deepened into a generalization about the human condition.

"Cold Iron" introduces us to a fading world of fantasy. Sir Huon and Lady Esclairmonde are the weaker successors of Oberon and Titania. They "crave to act and influence on folk in housen" (9). As it is, they can only tiptoe in and weave "a fag end of a charm here, or half spell there" (9) over the cradles of children who, when they grow up "act differently" from others of their station, which is "no advantage to man or maid." To Puck's suggestion that they take a child by fair dealing and make his fortune, as Oberon did in times past, Sir Huon replies sadly, "Time past is time past" (9). In what seems a last attempt to restore their waning power, they take the child of a dead slave woman and try to bring him up outside the human condition, "on the far side of Cold Iron." What follows is a diminuendo to the dream of a golden irresponsibility, of a surrender of wish fulfillment, and a demonstration of the insufficiency of fantasy. Against the lure of emotion, of the pity, for instance, that the boy feels for the woman beaten by her husband, the fairies have only illusions, "fresh shows, and plays, and magics to distract him from folk in housen" (17). They are pageants in the clouds, imagination without focus or the significance of real suffering or choice: "Behind them you could see great castles lifting slow and splendid on arches of moonshine, with maidens waving their hands at the windows, which all turned into roaring rivers; and then would come the darkness of his own young heart wiping out the whole slateful" (19). "Boy's magic," "shows and shadows for his mind to chew on," remain a shallow daydreaming without power to prevent the drift into boredom and irritable willfulness of an uninformed consciousness or "dark" mind. Only the choice of Cold Iron, of the law of service and sacrifice, offers an escape from empty distraction and illusion. Kipling's myth is a bold and original variant of the Fall motif of legend and folklore, found in those many stories which "explain" man's loss of *illo tempore* and his present bondage to time, work, suffering, and death. One significant difference between Kipling's variant and the usual treatment is that the dream life offered by Sir Huon and Lady Esclairmonde is artificial, self-defeating, and less, not more, than the human condition we know.

Kipling uses the god Thor as the image of that condition. The choice is interesting. Thor was not, like Odin, the champion of kings and nobles, but of craftsmen, peasants, and those who had to work. He was the maintainer of oaths and contracts. The power of the thunder, symbolized by his hammer Mjolinir, whose curved sign Puck makes in the air on mentioning Thor's name, was a "protection against evil and violence" (Davidson 1964, 84). The hammer, which was used to hallow marriage contracts, was sometimes supplemented, sometimes replaced, by a great ring, hence the significance of the iron ring in *Rewards and Fairies*. The god's power, resting largely on his immense physical strength, was extended over all that had to do with the well-being of the community: "Without it Asgard could no longer be guarded against the giants, men relied on it to give security and to support the rule of law" (84). Kipling is very little concerned with this strength and crude force of Thor. In particular, he does not emphasize the god's greatest exploit against the powers of darkness and evil: his defeat of the great Midgard serpent, Jormungand. This is all the more interesting since the victory of order over disorder is central to *Rewards and Fairies*. It is, besides, so essential to Thor and the many hero-gods of which he is a type: "A struggle to the death between a sky-god, guardian of men, and an appalling monster, hostile to men, is a commonplace of Indo-European mythology" (Crossley-Holland 1982, 208). Kipling prefers to see the victory of order over disorder not simply as one of strength but as one that must be purchased by pain and suffering. There is, then, the conflation in *Rewards and Fairies* of the worker-god Thor and the self-sacrificing Tyr, whose legend forms the basis of the second focal story in the collection, "The Knife and the Naked Chalk." The terrible wolf of the underworld allows himself to be bound as a game, but only on condition Tyr puts his hand into his mouth as a sign of good faith. When he finds he is imprisoned, Fenrir bites Tyr's hand off: "Tyr bravest of the gods twisted and cried out; unable and able to bear such pain. The other gods laughed, they knew that Fenrir was bound at last. They all laughed except Tyr; he lost his hand" (Crossley-Holland 1982, 36). Fenrir, like Thor's enemy Jormungand, is the offspring of the traitor god Loki. They are both extensions of the enemy within, the only enemy that "can affect and corrupt and finally destroy the spirit of the gods" (193).

Kipling clearly found certain qualities of the Norse gods imaginatively appealing in what seemed to him and his political circle a time of growing darkness and danger. These gods, as H. R. Ellis Davidson remarked, led dangerous individualistic lives, yet were part of a closely knit small group, "with a firm sense of values and certain intense loyalties" (1964, 86). It is very much the world of attitudes the reader meets throughout Kipling's stories. More noteworthy is the softening and deepening of the heroic attitude through the sacrificial pain of Tyr at which the gods laugh. The overtly "Christian" poem "Cold Iron" with which the story of the same name concludes only develops certain of the nuances already present in the Scandinavian material Kipling has selected. In the poem, "Cold Iron" modulates from the symbol of power worshipped by the baron who rebels against his lord to that of the suffering, sacrifice, and the forgiveness of the king he betrays, "Cold Iron out of Calvary."

What enriches the basic mythic framework is that, rather than imposing it as a recurring pattern, Kipling uses it to explore contradictory, not to say unpalatable, facts about loyalty and sacrifice. The most obvious and the most disturbing of these is the possibility that the object of one's sacrifice may be wholly unworthy of it. The second story in the collection, "Gloriana," raises this question in an acute form. The tale is prefaced by a skillful pastiche of an Elizabethan lyric, celebrating the readiness of the two cousins of "Gloriana" to die for their sovereign. The polished, rhythmically exquisite gestures of the poem are not subverted by the shabby facts of the story, but the two are thrown into an enigmatic contrast. At the heart of the Elizabethan legend and panache, Kipling places a pathologically treacherous, almost neurotic woman exploiting both patriotic loyalty and her own sexuality. The story is set in and grows out of the children's little fenced wood, "Willow Shaw," their "very own kingdom" (Kipling 1910, 31), which they "contrived to keep most particularly private." From this starting point, it explores, among other things, the implications of property, ownership, and responsibility—both what it means to protect and to guard and what it can do to the guardian. Queen Elizabeth, whom Puck summons before Dan and Una, is masked in black silk. The Spanish phrases with which she lards her conversion brilliantly suggest that she has come to partake of what she has spent her life fighting. She shares more with the muddy statecraft of her rival Philip of Spain than she does with the ardent youths she destroys.

Angus Wilson has criticized Kipling's Queen Elizabeth as a theatrical conception. In fact, the portrait is not so much a lifeless charade as a study of sterile artifice, of narcissistic cunning that may be justified by a *raison d'état* but that is damnable nevertheless. Every gesture Elizabeth makes is practiced, "her voice changed at each word" (34). She describes the incident recounted in "Gloriana" in terms of a play with herself as director: "You are to fancy the music on a sudden wavers away . . . Hsh! You mar the play" (39–40). Beneath the polished decor, the surface romance of Gloriana, Kipling suggests a frustrated sexuality: "Maids are often melancholic" (36). Elizabeth gloats, in an almost prurient fashion, over the "dainty youths," the "lively image of a brace of young cupids" (39), the "two lovely young sinners" (40) who are victims. She relishes the erotic undercurrent in her relationship with them and trades on it and on their nobility to send them to die in a forlorn expedition against a Spanish outpost.

One of the most striking features of the language of "Gloriana" is passages imitating sixteenth-century dance rhythms, which are also rhythms of imprisonment, convoluted and claustrophobic (38–39). Elizabeth thinks while she dances, and the dance echoes not only her dilemma but her mind and policy. The passages are a tour de force of suggestion and a perversion of one of the stock Tudor images, the dance as an image of cosmic harmony. The queen's almost obsessive references to acting pervert, in a somewhat similar fashion, the other favorite image of her time, the world as a stage. Kipling's enterprise in "Gloriana" is not the simple debunking of a famous figure. It is true that little of the romance of the Elizabethan age survives the close encounter with the queen, and the children are left shuddering and glad that Elizabeth is no longer there (50). Rather the story explores an impasse. The necessity for the cousins' sacrifice and death is real. Dan and Una are forced to admit that there was nothing else Elizabeth could do: "What else in England's name could she have done?" (46).

And yet, it is clear she enjoys her manipulations, revels in her perverse form of sexual blackmail and the pleasure of being a puppet master. What "Gloriana" insists on is that the twisted vileness of those who demand the necessary and tragic sacrifice cannot be used to argue away its necessity. The two facts simply exist together. There is no neat answer and the reaction of the bewildered, slightly frightened child ("I don't understand a bit" [45]) is the truest one.

The well-known verses with which the story ends echo, once more, the terrible dance rhythms in which the queen is imprisoned and that, curiously, she enjoys. The poem uses the legend, recorded in Agnes Strickland's popular and recently reprinted life, of the dying Elizabeth's seeing herself in a "true looking glass" for the first time in many years (1904, 355), as the image of her knowledge of her own damnation. Kipling wishes his childish audience to see, almost to the limits of what they can bear and understand, the corruption of power, the exploitation of the personal legend, even of sexual allure, the doing of the right thing for the wrong reason. It is necessary that they should see the worst that may be said about those political figures who demand sacrifice. They must see this and still see that the sacrifice is inescapable. "Gloriana," like other stories in *Rewards and Fairies,* is a kind of ordeal and a lesson of what it is to labor without hope of reward. Tyr must suffer the loss of his hand and the laughter of the gods. The suffering of Tyr and the laughter the victim must endure are equally present in the next tale but in a minor, almost a comic, key—as the mortification of pride and the good-humored acceptance of humiliation.

"The Wrong Thing" carries the reader into the world of those workmen who use the hammer of Thor. It is set in Mr. Springett's workshop, among ladders, "paints, pulleys and odds and ends" (57). The boy Dan pays the price of inattention as he cuts his finger while making a model ship. This sets the tone for the tale told by the visitor from the past, Hal o' the Draft, the Tudor wood-carver and builder. "The Wrong Thing" explores the inner motive for which one undertakes work, the surrender of self necessary to one's task. Hal is not, like the two cousins, called upon to sacrifice his life but to put aside pride, the expectation of reward or recognition, the consciousness of being an "artist." He learns from his master Torrigiano the discipline and sacrifice of work, the avoidance of the inchoate and tumid. The artist, or craftsman, is not a flamboyant egotist carelessly tossing off "a masterpiece" like the "great heaving play of dolphins" (68). Hal produces "all of a heat after supper." He is a disciple of Thor, god of journeymen, purifying his mind through the deliberate performance of simple tasks. In such a chastened, self-forgetting mood, Hal contributes the iron gates to Torrigiano's late-Gothic masterpiece, the tomb of Henry VII. Hal, however, must learn one final lesson about duty and sacrifice. He is knighted by the king, a dismal miser, not for his exquisite work on the tomb, but for providing his sovereign with a good excuse to save a small sum of money on a pleasure boat he promised to his mistress. The absurdity of his "honour," "the mad high humour of it" (75), dissipates the remains of his own self-regard and the envy of his deadly enemy Benedetto.

The second and third stories of *Reward and Fairies* have a common theme that is fairly easy to see. Both are about the condition of the effective sacrifice and the worthwhile work. The political powers they serve may be perverted like Elizabeth I or unbelievably petty-minded like Henry VII, but the chosen spirits of the elite do more than perform their tasks without hope of reward or recognition. They perform them with a graceful sanity and panache and an "honest craftsman's mirth" born of having reached the heavens of the higher levity, "earth's vanities, foreshortened and little" (76).

At first sight, "Marklake Witches" seems a radical break with the stories that precede it. "Gloriana" and "The Wrong Thing" are clearly and intimately linked, tragic and comic slants on the same subject. The reader might be excused for thinking "Marklake Witches," by contrast, simply an exercise in creating period or ambience, the age of sensibility, or a handling, in a minor key, of the theme of the far better known "They," that of the death of children. This was, of course, a deeply personal theme for Kipling, who never quite recovered from the death of his daughter Josephine. "Marklake Witches" is, in fact, closely integrated into the subtly textured total effect of *Rewards and Fairies*.

In part, the story is about an art of dying nobly, a way of making death—and, much more, tragically foreshortened life—not merely bearable but significant and valuable. It is far easier to understand sacrifice and duty, the bondage of cold iron, as terms applied to a heroic exploit, or even an excellently managed piece of work by a craftsman or an artist, than to see their relevance to the brief life of a forgotten child. The point is emphasized since a girl like Philadelphia seems to have no role in the man's world of revolutionary wars.

"Marklake Witches" uses the doomed child not only as a focus of love but, more importantly, of the healing of divisions. Around the fragile, evanescent figure of Philadelphia are reconciled, at least locally, the most violently opposed forces of her time: France and England, nations at war, and the revolutionary and conservative ideologies that they espouse. More than Jerry, Philadelphia is the true "witch" of the story. She draws together the medical orthodoxy of Dr. Break, the wisdom enshrined in the folklore and popular culture of the witchmaster Jerry, and the somewhat arrogant innovativeness of the French prisoner René, inventor of a rudimentary stethoscope.

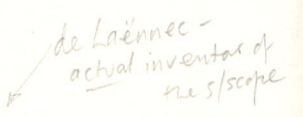

"Marklake Witches" is intended to be exemplary. It is linked to Una's situation and development as "The Wrong Thing" had been linked to those of Dan. Both stories are about learning. In each the "lesson" is introduced or reinforced by physical pain: Dan's cutting his thumb, the blow in Una's face from the tail of the cow she is trying to milk. Both little incidents reinforce the notion of work and of life as disciplines in which carelessness or inattention bring their penalty.

Superficially, the striking of this opening note does not seem to relate to Philadelphia, with her flighty, imperious tone and all the airs and graces of the squire's indulged daughter. Part of her poignance, however, lies in the contrast the reader is meant to see between the manner of the "little madam" and the reality of what she feels and half knows, her own inevitable death, between the surface appearance of a headstrong girl and Philadelphia's *actions,* which all stem from care and responsibility for her father, whose happiness and comfort she tries to secure; for René, whom she rescues from prison; for her old servant Cissie, caught stealing; even for Dr. Break. But there is a deeper contrast than this. It is made clear when Philadelphia eavesdrops on René and Jerry as they discuss her hopeless state of health. Kipling intends his readers to see, not the simple pathos of the dying innocent, but a deeper intuition that informs all Philadelphia's acts of healing. Dr. Elizabeth Kübler-Ross, one of the most interesting investigators of the psychology of dying children, remarks that

> children are very much easier than adults. Naturally, the younger they are, the less they are contaminated by us, the less they have picked up our fears and anxieties. Children, human beings, consist of a physical emotional intellectual quadrant. A five-year-old child with a brain tumour does not understand intellectually what a brain stem is, but that child because of the physical quadrant deteriorating, develops very early, say ten years too early, a spiritual quadrant, an intuitive quadrant. (1984, 8)

Philadelphia does not appear to admit to her conscious mind the fact of her own dying condition, but her intuition of it colors all her actions. In any case, terms like "knowledge" and "conscious mind" are too crude to fit the case. They violate the child's awareness of her coming death as much as the nature of her dawning love for René, inevitably to live "but for an hour" (111). Yet the squire's daughter has her "triumph" (110) won by her jaunty courage, cheerfulness, and love for those about her. Kipling's point here is that duty and sacrifice, keeping oneself full of high spirits and generosity yet absolute for death, are a way of giving distinction to the passing of a few forgotten years. The very way through the woods on which the girl rode has been erased.

Yet the poem "Brookland Road," with which "Marklake Witches" concludes, suggests that the discipline Philadelphia instinctively, or perhaps knowingly, imposed on herself colored the lives of those who remained. Her life was not without effect. She entered the closed circle of other minds and united those divided from each other in love of herself. "I was very pleased with what I knowed / I reckoned myself no fool — / Till I met a maid on the Brookland Road / That turned me back to school" (113). The loss of such a choice spirit as the squire's daughter can break hearts yet open minds to sympathy and fellow feeling. "Marklake Witches" is, besides, an important stage in the emotional development encouraged by *Rewards and Fairies*. It tentatively offers a way to cope with the fear of death and the even more insidious resentment at the injustice of the life cut off. Una at the beginning of the tale complains how "unfair" it is that the cow's tail should hit her. At the end, she asks cheerfully, "What's going to hurt me?" (112). She has understood a finer level of conduct.

Rewards and Fairies may be indeed viewed as a conduct book, suggesting various aspects of, or insights into, the elevated and noble way of life Kipling wishes to recommend to the young who may one day wield power or influence. It is obvious that Dan and Una are being taught. It is also worth keeping in mind the notion of a journey. The issues involved and the problems posed grow increasingly dark and vexed, especially in the middle section and at the end of *Rewards and Fairies*. The reader is carefully led by stages, with adequate preparation, into more and more troubling matters that, nevertheless, he or she must know about. Apart from the book's other excellent qualities, Kipling's handling of his relationship with the growing child calls for special admiration. This delicacy and tact in the handling of a perplexing matter are specially evident in the next story, the moral complement to "Cold Iron."

"The Knife and the Naked Chalk," which follows "Marklake Witches," marks a return to the overtly mythic level. The figure of Thor introduced *Rewards and Fairies*. The less familiar Tyr guides the reader into its darker reaches. The story is set on the Sussex Downs, which the children find far less interesting, almost without features, compared with the lush, thickly wooded Weald. In a superb passage describing their eddying movement of air (122), Kipling creates a multiplying sense of the life, movement, beauty and sheer variety of these apparently sterile and monotonous uplands. This empty, quiet countryside visited only by shepherds like Mr. Dudeney and tourists has its own authentic character. More than this, it was once the scene of one of the most vital of all events in unrecorded history, man's defeat of the wolf, the precondition of all subsequent human development in the British Isles. This was a slow victory won by "many men through the years, each working in his own country," and by the weapons of Thor, "hand, hammer and spear" (124). "The Knife and the Naked Chalk" deals with much more than a mere physical victory over a dangerous enemy. Among its more essential themes is the advance toward order as the result of initiation, at a price, into a higher state of knowledge. The man of the New Stone Age whom Puck introduces to the children shares his people's fear of that knowledge, which can never be merely a new technology but must involve a new state of consciousness.

The ironworkers of the Weald do not have an overtly hostile relationship to the flint-workers of the Downs. The two peoples leave each other alone. However, the more advanced culture of those who live in the shadows under the great trees that are one of Thor's emblems is, of necessity, and without the need of physical conquest, destructive of the identity of the more primitive people. The stone-age man explains that "the Children of the Night, though they worship our Gods, are magicians. When a man goes into their country, they change his spirit; they put words into his mouth; they make him like talking water" (128). The point he makes seems to mean that the more technologically advanced people are also more articulate, askers of many questions that they do not give one time to answer (131). The superior ability of the Children of Night to articulate and to conceptualize explains the flint-worker's fear that after visiting them, he would not know whether he would return in his own shape (129). This is indeed the case. When he returns to his own people the flint-worker finds he has lost that intuitive understanding of their thoughts and feelings he had once possessed: "Their hearts are changed. I cannot see into their hearts as I used to" (134–35).

"The Knife and the Naked Chalk" explores some of the themes dealt with much later in Golding's *The Inheritors*. There are significant differences, however. Kipling is concerned with the need as well as the pain of an evolving consciousness. The Children of the Night will only give some of their iron knives, with which alone the wolves can be defeated, on condition that the flint-worker, as a proof of his sincerity, agrees to have one of his eyes put out. This is a precise metaphor for a necessary narrowing of consciousness. When the flint-worker first came into contact with the Children of the Night, he succumbed to a feverish illness, with undertones of a nervous breakdown. On one level this collapse has affinities with the ritual "death" found in many primitive initiation rites. More significant, however, is the connection established between painful sacrifice and surrender of part of himself, symbolized by the loss of an eye, and certain strands of Norse myth. When he returns to his people with the knives, "they said I was the son of Tyr, the God who put his right hand in the Beast's mouth" (136). There is a suggestion too, of a link with one-eyed Odin, who sacrificed his eye and hung upon the tree Yggdrasil to secure knowledge and understanding.

The wildly anachronistic identification with Tyr serves two purposes. It makes the trauma of new knowledge and of culture shock bearable by reference to an ancient mythic prototype. When the tribe think him "to be a God like the God Tyr, who gave his hand to conquer a Great Beast" (136), they identify the nature of his role and sacrifice in a pattern or religious scheme that may be half-forgotten but that lies at the basis of human experience. Though not often recalled, it is a bedrock of understanding. Significantly, the tribe hail him as Tyr in the "Old Tongue" (137), which the priestesses use when they make prayers to the Old Dead in the barrows. The flint-worker's apotheosis is also symbolic of the imprisonment of the leader, inventor, and discoverer. He must sacrifice an ordinary private life. Nothing is left for him but "the words and the songs and the worship" (138).

"The Knife and the Naked Chalk" grows out of, and yet transcends, those political allegiances which produced "Below the Mill Dam." Among the strongest concerns of those right-wing Tories of whom Kipling was the spokesman was the question of Britain's refusal to adapt to technological change. "National Efficiency" was a fairly common slogan or watchword in the opening years of the twentieth century. It grew out of a perception of the need to accept new technology, industrial techniques, and more effective administrative machinery and for specific measures like the conscription Kipling portrayed in "The Army of a Dream." Although most commonly associated with Kipling's hero Milner, "efficiency" was taken up by the right wing of the Liberal Party under Lord Rosebery. "The Knife and the Naked Chalk" moves away from the mere ridicule of the antiscientific mandarins in "Below the Mill Dam" to a profound consideration of the issues involved in the search for "efficiency" at any time. The pain, the loneliness, the loss, and the certainty that "all new things are sorrow" (129) exist in an enigmatic tension with the necessity to undergo change. The enemy, The Beast, is more than the physical danger of the actual wolf. It is something insidious and sadistic (126), destructive of man's dignity and sense of identity: "To fight the Beast is nothing, but to be despised by The Beast when he fights you—that is like his teeth in your heart" (127). If societies or individuals refuse to develop, they do not remain static but fall prey to Fenrir, the brutal force that negates and belittles all human effort. The Beast can only be overcome by pain and sacrifice.

Many accounts of Kipling's artistic development have emphasized the effect of the First World War and of his son's death. It has been frequently suggested that these public and private tragedies and his own experience of increasing physical pain and loneliness deepened Kipling's understanding of suffering and of the sacrifice that is the price of order and of "overcoming the Beast." In studying his evolution, however, it is important to give due weight to *Rewards and Fairies*. Kipling in *Something of Myself* says almost more about it than any other of his books, implying its artistic sophistication in speaking of the problem of devising a complex and subtle tone of "three or four overlaid tints and textures," in a work suitable both for adults and children (1990, 111). Although characteristically reticent and cryptic when mentioning anything personal, he leaves the reader in no doubt that he viewed *Rewards and Fairies* as a turning point in his writing, "A sort of balance to, as well as a seal upon, my 'Imperialistic' output in the past" (111). Kipling seems to imply that *Rewards and Fairies* both sums up tendencies found in his earlier work and, at the same time, contains new moral and psychological perceptions that he wishes to set against those he had previously stressed.

The reader is likely to agree with Kipling's own assessment. Duty, suffering, and sacrifice were, of course, found in his work from the beginning. In the earlier books, however, their moral dimension is relatively underplayed. *Captains Courageous* (1896–97) is concerned with the character-forming effect of hardship, but at the level of physical discomfort, a necessary toughening of mind and body. The whole collection *The Day's Work* (1898) celebrates the discipline of self-sacrificing labor convincingly and pleasingly. Yet its moral scheme remains simple. One gives all one can to one's work and therefore enjoys it to the full. In *Kim* (1900–1901) the sacrifice and suffering that promote spiritual growth and the "great Game," the resourceful and cunning battle of government against disorder, simply exist on two quite separate planes. Kim reverences the lama and his quest, but he does not feel any need to imitate him at the end of the book.

2 / *Rewards and Fairies:* Thor and Tyr

It is probable that the watershed is passed in Kipling's work between 1906 and 1910 rather than around 1915. In *Puck of Pook's Hill* dutifulness in the Norman, if not the Roman, cycle is *rewarded* by a confident, developing civilization and a growth of freedom under law. In *Rewards and Fairies* suffering must simply be born. It *may* be fruitful, but there is no promise of this. This is what is involved in the substitution of Thor and Tyr for Weland. It was a change that Kipling made deliberately and consciously. As he suggests in *Something of Myself,* he wanted a new departure in his work. He chose to change on the principle of the "Old Law": "As soon as you find you can do anything, do something you can't" (1990, 111).

3

Rewards and Fairies:
Loyalty and Sacrifice

Rewards and Fairies, even more than its predecessor of four years before, *Puck of Pook's Hill,* raises, in a peculiarly acute form, one of the perennial problems of Kipling's work: the contrast between the imaginative artist and the political "thinker." The period from the Liberal landslide of 1906 to the First World War was for Kipling, his biographers agree, one of tension and mounting anger (Carrington 1970, 474–77; Wilson 1977, 232–33). The paltering away, as he saw it, of Britain's victory in the South African war, the disgrace of Lord Milner, the advance of the trade unions and socialism, the weak surrender of the House of Lords to advancing democracy, and many other signs of the times drove him into a state bordering on chronic fury. His increasing bitterness culminated in a notorious speech in May 1914 at Tunbridge Wells, in which he associated himself with current demands by the right wing of the Tory Party for violent physical resistance to the Asquith government's plans for Irish home rule.

Angus Wilson has pointed out how discussion of Kipling's political response to the social and moral tensions and transitions before 1914 has been rendered difficult and embarrassing. The "corporatism" of the radical Right of the Edwardian Tory party, of Joseph Chamberlain, Leo Amery, and others, which Kipling espoused, seems to have had features that "in their later European forms . . . accrued enormities so detestable to our generations" (Wilson 1977, 241). Needless to say, this appearance of embryonic Fascism is a misreading. Orwell's definitive essay long ago distinguished between the position of an Edwardian imperialist and right-wing Tory of around 1910 and a Fascist of the 1930s (Orwell 1966, 179–81). Perhaps it is surprising such a misconception should ever have arisen, let

3 / *Rewards and Fairies:* Loyalty and Sacrifice

alone that it still persists in some quarters. However, Kipling's political views cannot be simply ignored in discussing the period in his career during which *Rewards and Fairies* was written.

Critics are inclined now to discriminate more intelligently between various aspects of Kipling's most overt phase of political involvement. The radical Right's diagnosis of, and solutions for, Britain's social and moral crisis were clearly faulty in many respects. (Wilson [1977, 241] reminds us, rightly, of its failure to understand economics.)

Nevertheless, both the diagnosis and the solutions were deeply felt and often incidentally brilliant. Kipling and his mentors felt that they were facing an immense danger. George Dangerfield's long-established, retrospective analysis of this "crisis" and his view that only the First World War saved Britain from governmental collapse and social upheaval have been subjected to some revision. Recent historical writing, perhaps as a useful corrective, has been inclined to stress the stability and continuity of Edwardian ideas and institutions. Revisionism, however, has certainly not carried the day. Alan O'Day remarks, in a collection of essays by writers on the period, that although none of them agrees with the *details* of the picture of disintegration painted by Dangerfield in *The Strange Death of Liberal England,* most of them "do provide substantial support for his brushwork" (O'Day 1979, 2).

Whatever view may be taken in hindsight, the radical Right, and Kipling as their foremost literary representative, had no doubt of the scale, or of the essential features, of the impending catastrophe. One of the most significant of these features, from the use he made of it imaginatively, was the fear of a failure of leadership in the ruling class of his country. Some of his best known and finest political allegories, written at this time of anxiety, make the point explicitly. "Below the Mill Dam" (in *Traffics and Discoveries*), like the "Song of the Old Guard," with its refrain, "Hey then up go we!," attacks an elite that does no work in exchange for its privileges, and that resists technological development and institutional efficiency in the name of a limp and ineffectual tradition. The speeches of the Cat, the Rat, and the Wheel, before they are swept away by the torrents of change, are a parody, instantly recognizable and murderously funny, of the airs and graces of the indolent litterateur A. J. Balfour, who led the Tory party till 1911, and of the Tory establishment.

In "The Mother Hive" (in *Actions and Reactions*), of the year before *Rewards and Fairies,* the wax moth, a parasite and type of the specious liberal intellectual who infiltrates and destroys the society of the hive, is relatively insignificant. She has no power of her own, any more than Kipling's earlier representatives of her kind: the Bandar-log, chattering, self-deceiving monkeys, as liberal intellectuals are represented in the Mowgli stories. The weight in "The Mother Hive" falls on the weakness and irresolution of those who should have guarded the state.

The radical Right certainly did not question privilege or the hierarchical basis of society. What Kipling and the faction with which he was associated felt, however, was that privilege must be earned by service, self-sacrifice, efficiency, and a loyalty extending even to death. Without such qualities, the elite becomes merely ornamental, like the old mill and its inhabitants. Both the standard histories and the best-known memoirs of the pre-1914 period suggest how prevalent crude versions of an ethic of patriotic self-abnegation were in the public schools (Marwick 1967, 26–27). In Kipling's political satires it is altogether sharper and more intelligent, the vehicle of an acute social criticism. Nothing in "Below the Mill Dam" and "The Mother Hive," however, prepares the reader for the subtlety with which Kipling handles the themes of loyalty, work, and sacrifice in *Rewards and Fairies*.

The title, with its echo of Richard Corbet's verses, evokes a sterner mood than that of *Puck of Pook's Hill*. Unlike Charles I's bishop of Oxford, however, Kipling is not lamenting the passing of picturesque superstitions and rural charm under the onset of puritanism and rationalism. The title is more limited and literal in its application. What is being surrendered, among other things, is the expectation that good is *rewarded*, that stories will end happily. *Rewards and Fairies* deals with a delicate point of transition, the passing from "the chamber of maiden thought" in Keats's phrase, the exchange of the pleasures of fancy for the weight of an often sorrowful reality.

This putting away of childish things is, more than most, a topic rich in opportunities for humbug and heavy-handedness, for labored contrasts between childish dreaming and adult responsibilities. It lends itself to moralizings, whether about "duty" in Kipling's day or "maturity" in ours. Apart from any other qualities, *Rewards and Fairies* is an outstanding example of literary tact, the skillful handling of a potentially intractable theme.

A substantial part of this success stems from the manipulation of the myth that underlies the stories, and from the strength of that myth in carrying what one may crudely call the "message." As I have suggested earlier, Kipling adapts a thread of imagery drawn from Scandinavian legend to carry the meanings of *Rewards and Fairies*. The myths of Thor and Tyr are

3 / *Rewards and Fairies:* Loyalty and Sacrifice

as boldly refracted through the medium of his mind and art, and bent as much to his purpose, as the strikingly different Scandinavian fable of Weland and his sword had been in *Puck of Pook's Hill.* However, there are certain tales in the collection where the myths of Thor and Tyr are not so dominant or—perhaps more accurately—where the mythic motifs of sacrifice and sufferings are viewed from an odd angle, and where the awkward but natural reservations about them are allowed to surface.

The key questions about concepts like "loyalty" and "sacrifice" must always be "Why?" and "For what?" How is the worthy object of loyalty to be discovered? Kipling does not balk at the problem but deals with it in two connected stories, "Brother Square-Toes" and "A Priest in Spite of Himself." The first tale is prefaced, interestingly, by the poem "Philadelphia," whose jaunty rhythms and wry humor contrast with the poignance of its theme, the loss of the past:

> If you're off to Philadelphia in the morning,
> You mustn't take my stories for a guide.
> There's little left indeed of the city you will read of,
> And all the folk I write about have died. . . .

All the particular details of the eighteenth-century America the story is to create have vanished. Yet, nurtured by Washington's prudence, the new society has survived:

> I pledge my word you'll find the pleasant land behind
> Unaltered since Red Jacket rode that way. . . .

The landscape, symbol of "the things that truly last, when men and times have passed," is still there to inspire the visitor.

Pharaoh Lee, the Gypsy and smuggler who is the hero of the two pieces, could not have been better chosen to illustrate an alternative morality or counterculture. Half French and half English, his family cannot understand the struggle of nations at war. Why can't French and English "fight it out" (Kipling 1910, 151) over their heads? The curious yet revealing manner in which Pharaoh joins the navy of revolutionary France, after leaping through the open porthole of a French ship, suggests a man who can glide over the surface of societies and ideologies because he feels no loyalty to them. They are not of ultimate value to him, and he can play off one against another. "An all-Englishman might have been shocked—but that's where my French blood saved me" (154). Morally, he stands at an odd angle to the world. Both sides of his family are hereditary smugglers, "brought up to the trade . . . same as fiddling" (149).

The description of the young Pharaoh's arrival in the United States evokes the sheer physical beauty of Pennsylvania, starting with the first scent of the lilacs. Kipling contrasts the boy's response to this beauty, the reality of "looking and smelling and touching" (155), with the milling crowds, gripped by a factitious war fever, harangued by the French ambassador:

> I couldn't make sense of it. I wanted to get out from that crunch of swords and petticoats and sit in a field. (155)

Pharaoh's "primitive" or Gypsy consciousness relishes every original, spare, strange detail of the new scene and of the people into whose company he is thrown. The "smell of cheese and medicines fit to knock you down" (156–57), the musical clock on the wall of Toby's shop (158), the little room behind the oven, looking onto the flower garden where Pharaoh slept at Conrad Gerhard's (159), the "brass chandeller you could see your face in" at the Moravian Church (160)—all have a rich particularity, a sense of surprise, a life in them. Yet, as "Brother Square-Toes" makes clear, it is the irreplaceable atmospheres, the special and peculiar ambiences, the rare and unusual cultures, that are liable to be destroyed by "national crusades," manifest destinies, and crowd hysteria.

Kipling emphasizes the point by casting his Gypsy lad as a kind of noble savage in reverse, coming as observer from the Old World to the New, among two sets of people who were, perhaps, quite unusual even in late-eighteenth-century America. The Moravian Brethren and their Seneca Indian converts are not part of the "movement of history"—unlike the French ambassador Genet and his revolutionary ideology. They do not serve to prove any kind of point, are not in modern jargon "relevant." They were unique and precious, but are now "gone with lost Atlantis." Yet they, and such as they, would have been prematurely dragged down by a wholly unnecessary popular war.

When Cornplanter and the other Senecas go to their secret rendezvous with Washington to learn his decision, "they knew well, if there was war 'twixt England and the United States, their tribe 'ud catch it from both parties same as in all the other wars" (166). When Big Hand assures the Indian chiefs that he will not sanction war against England they thank him with a significant ceremony. Wearing regalia so colorful that it is "making the very leaves look silly" (166), they bow before the president, "looking like jewelled images" (171): "It's the Sachems' way of sprinkling the sacred corn-meal in front of—oh! it's a piece of Indian compliment. . . ." (171–72).

It is in fact the way to honor a god, and a hint of that crossing of the frontier of the supernatural suggested elsewhere in *Rewards and Fairies*, most directly through the myths of Thor and Tyr. The appearance of the godlike is always associated with duty and sacrifice.

The poem "If—" that ends "Brother Square-Toes," though familiar to the point of being hackneyed, is enriched and explained by its reference to Washington in the preceding story. The aging president is no longer the heroic, admired leader of the War of Independence but a figure whose prudence and statesmanship seem to thwart national pride and self-consciousness. "If—" does not celebrate some *obviously* masterful man as it superficially appears to do, but one who in the trough of unpopularity and the ebb of his physical strength tells the unwelcome truth, or makes the decision that has no evident glamour. Washington's sacrifice is to ride through a jeering mob because he will not strike the easy attitudes they want. Peace, however, though it lacks excitement, is what the new country needs, not a popular war, "she having but so few years back wound up one against England, and being all holds full of her own troubles" (170). The counterpart to "If—," the false heroic against the true, is the immediately following "St. Helena Lullaby," whose childish rhythm reduces the career of the egocentric Napoleon to a sad little pattern of inevitability.

Taken together, the two stories told by Pharaoh Lee chart his growth of loyalty and of "belonging." This is not a conventional patriotism imposed from above, but one rooted in his own aesthetic and moral sense. Several influences are brought to bear on him. There is a response, initially and perhaps always essentially physical, to the rightness and comeliness of the Moravians' way of life with its "clean strangeness" (160), to which he becomes a somewhat wayward convert. There is, too, the beauty of the Pennsylvania countryside where sense impressions, the smell of the wild grape and the sound of the catbird, modulate gradually into the celebration of a moral idyll. Pharaoh journeys with his Indian friends, "a seemly, quiet people" (162), through an enchanted, almost a sanctified landscape, "tacking from one place to another—such as Lancaster, Bethlehem-Ephrata—'thou Bethlehem-Ephrata'" (161–62). Having glimpsed this peaceable kingdom, he understands the weight of Washington's sacrifice, the sad determined sanity that keeps it in peace.

Most important of all is the force of example. Pharaoh moves from admiration of the Indians' hunting skills and colorful costumes to a liking for their grave self-sufficient manners: "Indians don't ask questions much and I wanted to be like 'em" (164). They trust him to remain silent when he holds their horses during the secret meeting with Washington, and that trust marks the real turning point in his moral career. The free-floating Gypsy boy has found that to which he must be true, and for which he, in turn, must sacrifice.

The sequel to "Brother Square-Toes," "A Priest in Spite of Himself," shows the effect of Pharaoh Lee's choice of the moral life and the way in which his new loyalty ripples outward in a curious and unexpected fashion. The acts of duty and sacrifice possess a redemptive power beyond anything that might be predicted and move in strange ways to perform their miracles. Pharaoh refuses to betray the secret of Washington's decision to keep America out of the war to the ex-bishop and revolutionary politician in exile, Talleyrand.

Kipling's portrait of this man is a feat equal to the re-creation of life on the Roman Wall in *Puck of Pook's Hill*. It is not the comforting picture painted in Duff Cooper's until recently standard life of Talleyrand (1932). Cooper concentrates on the subtle realism of Talleyrand's policies, and the charm of his manners, to sketch a gentle, mellow figure whose effect on his time is hard to understand. Kipling, faced by the same moral ambivalence and tangled skein of facts, starts from the effects of power and fear. "He is bad," says Red Jacket. "But he is a great chief" (Kipling 1910, 187).

When he sees Talleyrand by chance, alone, playing dice one hand against the other, Pharaoh wonders "that even those dead dumb dice 'ud dare to fall different from what that face wished" (187). Talleyrand, along with Napoleon and Washington, is one of the three men in the world "who are quite by themselves" (191–92). His nature combines a terrible willpower with a rationality that possesses the knowledge of good and evil. Sinning, when he sins, knowingly and against the light, the ex-bishop understands what virtue and loyalty are when they are presented to his cold scrutiny. The moment (194–95) when the schemer is brought face to face with the boy's faith is one of the strangest in *Rewards and Fairies*. It gains by being reported with that loaded economy practiced in Kipling's later work, at length, in such masterpieces as "Mrs Bathurst" (in *Traffics and Discoveries*) and "Dayspring Mishandled" (in *Limits and Renewals*). The incident

3 / *Rewards and Fairies:* Loyalty and Sacrifice

is left mysterious, with no attempt at facile psychological explanation. When Talleyrand dismisses Washington as "that estimable old man," Pharaoh replies, "The Red Skin said that when thee hast met the President thee will feel in thy heart he is a stronger man than thee" (195).

Talleyrand tells the boy to go before he should kill him. When, however, he returns to France he leaves Pharaoh a gift of £100 and an ambiguous promise that "If ever we meet again you may be sure that I will do my best to repay what I owe you" (196–97). Several years later, when he is Napoleon's chief adviser, he sees to it that Pharaoh, now a merchant, has a cargo returned to him that had been seized by privateers belonging to the French branch of his own family.

Though the reader is left to work out his own interpretation of these events, a general direction may be discerned. Talleyrand may simply be grateful for the food the Moravian Brethren gave him. Clearly, however, there is more involved. "A Priest in Spite of Himself" is so called because he was initially forced into holy orders by his family. Yet this coercion, which embittered and twisted his nature, imparted a grace that he cannot reject. By virtue of his unwished-for calling, Talleyrand must know the godlike when he sees it. Through his priestly office, he must recognize the divine. What the Indians saw when they bowed before Washington, Talleyrand sees in the Gypsy boy's faith and duty. He hates yet admires it.

Rightly, *Rewards and Fairies* does not keep on one level. Before a final return to mystery and awe in "The Tree of Justice," Kipling deliberately lightens the book's tone. "The Conversion of St. Wilfrid," "A Doctor of Medicine," and "Simple Simon" are sensitive, and skillfully told, but in each case meaning is not far to seek. The first story, set during the conversion of the English in the seventh century, deals with the withdrawing or transferring of loyalty, and the conditions of such a withdrawal. It pursues the theme of the converter who learns from those he converts, a theme explored much more fully in the late stories centered on St. Paul and the rise of Christianity—"The Manner of Men" and "The Church that was at Antioch." Kipling, in "The Conversion of St. Wilfrid" as in these later works, is concerned with the curious symbiotic relationship of the old with the new faith. The new loyalty must be prepared to take something from the old, and to make its peace with it. Norse paganism in this story is in its twilight, rejected by intelligent men like the landowner and minor chieftain Meon, a scholar and brilliant talker (228–29). It cannot satisfy the intellect and, more damaging, is corroded by its inherent fatalism, exemplified by the South Saxons' readiness to give up life when it becomes boring:

> When they grew tired of life (as if they were the only people) they would jump into the sea. They called it going to Wotan. (227)

Christianity, on its side, is not reconciled with nature unsanctified. St. Wilfrid, and still more his acolyte Eddi, is suspicious of Meon's pet seal Padda, "a child of the Devil" (231). The seal, whose tricks the priests think diabolical, represents for his complex, bitter, unhappy master a glimpse of unconditional loyalty: "He can't tell a lie, and he doesn't know how to love anyone except me" (231). Meon does not find such loyalty among men.

In the key incident of the story (236), St. Wilfrid advises the pagan not to desert his fathers' gods to save his life, when they are both in danger. The obvious, if crucial, point is that loyalty is not bought, is not conditional on some benefit received, and may not be withdrawn when no longer advantageous. Meon is converted by the bishop's affirmation of unconditional loyalty, the need to keep one's faith even if one may save one's soul by breaking faith. But Wilfrid too is converted. The appearance of Padda through the waves (236) to the trapped men exemplifies such loyalty, and at the same time breaks through the Christian suspicion of nature unsanctified. Eddi's "Oh, blessing be on thee, my little brother Padda!" (237) anticipates St. Francis. The moment of passage between pagan and Christian is eased. If the Pharaoh Lee cycle explores the complex ways in which loyalties are formed, this simpler tale suggests that the moment when they are severed must be honorable.

"A Doctor of Medicine" contributes another nuance to the overall theme of *Rewards and Fairies*. "An Astrologer's Song," which opens the piece, states the paradox that a superstitious mode of thought may inspire hope and right action—

> Up, heart, and be cheerful,
> And lustily sing:
> *What chariot, what horses,*
> *Against us shall bide*
> *While the Stars in their courses*
> *Do fight on our side?*
>
> (251)

Astrology was a vehicle of confidence and courage because it grew from a determination that nature was ordered and rational, that it would give answers if questions were put to it. Even if the model of the universe through which men operated was untrue, it would still, given loyalty and

3 / *Rewards and Fairies:* Loyalty and Sacrifice

sacrifice, be the means of quelling fear. The Puritan doctor Culpeper's faithfulness to his Royalist patients cuts across the ideological division of the Civil War. His loyalty to them, and surrender, in their interests, of his own political and religious prejudices, is far more important than his discovery, through a bizarre train of astrological "reasoning," of the right way to deal with the plague.

In "Simple Simon," Kipling stands at an oblique angle to received historical impressions in order to glance at a somewhat unusual area in which loyalty and sacrifice operate. The friendship of Simon, the burgess of Rye, and Sir Francis Drake is an instance of Romance and its underpinnings, of the ways in which outstanding careers, brilliant and famous achievements, glorious eras, and the exploits we have heard of rest on the day-to-day work of ordinary people of whom we do not hear. Historically, Kipling's intuition here is as sound and searching as it is in the far more famous picture of the Roman Wall in *Puck of Pook's Hill*. Many subsequent authorities have suggested that the Elizabethan glory was inseparable from the solid virtues and professional competence of the late-sixteenth-century middle class. In more general terms, "Simple Simon" is well attuned to the themes of *Rewards and Fairies,* the hard work and practical skill of Thor, god of those who labor at a trade. These are the virtues that Kipling and his political allies saw the ruling class of 1910 as most needing—the hard, slogging grind needed to gain technical expertise.

During the earlier part of "Simple Simon," Drake is not the dashing pirate or the great commander of the world voyage, but a tradesman learning his craft in obscure encounters and dangerous and dirty episodes of guerrilla war off the Dutch coast:

An' what was his tools? A coaster boat—a liddle box o' walty plankin' an' some few fathom feeble rope held together an' made able by *him* sole. (290)

The significant word *tools* here, and the concluding poem, "Frankie's Trade," emphasize the workaday hardships of the great captain's apprenticeship on dark nights in the North Sea.

>   I learned him his trade o' winter nights,
>   'Twixt Mardyk Fort and Dunkirk lights
>   On a five-knot tide with the forts a-firing.
>   *(All round the Sands!)*

Before success comes the Gods of the Copybook Headings must be served, and "every man born of woman has his log to shift" (285).

It is while Drake serves out his years of learning his "trade" that he cements his friendship with "Simple Simon," who will later pursue his own course of obscure respectability. Kipling does not intend the reader to see Simon as a mental defective, but merely as a man of unusual good-humored straightforwardness bordering on naivety, "his brown eyes . . . as soft as a spaniel's" (282). Among all their visitors, he is the one the children respond to most warmly (289).

The curious, unrecorded friendship of this ordinary man with the extraordinary Drake seems, for Kipling, to exemplify so much that, although vital, can never be known about the background to great historical denouements, the faces in the shadows around the heroes and the superman. In his years of suffering, dodging Spanish ships in the storm and off the sandbanks of the Dutch coast, it is clear that Drake begins to doubt himself, and comes near to despair. He reveals this to Simon with that lack of warning which is one of the riskiest and generally one of the most successful of Kipling's narrative strategies. Suddenly, as they lean over the side of the ship, Drake asks, "Do you ever feel minded to jump overside and be done with everything?" (294). Simon's reply is not a ringing affirmation but a purely practical point: "No. What water comes aboard is too wet as 'tis." Through this curious, understated encounter of the famous with the obscure, Drake is, in a manner, reconciled to his fate.

This reconciliation is enforced by a reciprocal act of sacrifice in which both men join. Drake must embrace the brilliant but bitter future, including the necessary execution of his best friend, Doughty, as foretold by Simon's aunt. "Simple Simon" Cheyney must, in his turn, embrace the "ordinary" world on which the heroic is reared. He must give up his dream of ships made of iron. They may one day sail the seas, but the time is not ripe for them. In the meantime, the work of the day must fit the need of the day. As his aunt tells him, "Your duty's to your town and trade now" (295).

There is an objection to any patterning of experience, any attempt to fit life into a schema—even one so diverse in its examples, so multifarious in its imaginative power, so refreshingly full of changes of tone as Kipling's in *Rewards and Fairies*. The mind rebels against the formula. Surely, it feels, this cannot be all. Surely duty and sacrifice cannot be the whole of life. Kipling, however, anticipates Lawrence's dictum that every great work of art contains within itself the materials out of which a criticism of its

3 / *Rewards and Fairies:* Loyalty and Sacrifice

vision might be made. Among its many virtues is the fact that *Rewards and Fairies* is not morally restrictive.

The final story of the collection, "The Tree of Justice," brings the reader to the limits of the schema the other stories have explored. Kipling does not intend to devalue the moral pattern he has established, nor even to show its relativity. Although, of course, the tone is very different, the effect of the placing of "The Tree of Justice" in *Rewards and Fairies* is somewhat similar to the existence of the "two sides" of Kim's head. Totally different moral universes or schemes of value—the Great Game and the Search for the River of the Arrow in *Kim*—do not contradict each other. There is no suggestion that Kim must make an irrevocable choice between them. They simply represent different planes on which life may be understood. All that can be said is that both are valid and that Kim needs both. So, having enforced the need for duty and sacrifice, *Rewards and Fairies* ends with a tale that, taking one who refused both the duty and the sacrifice, insists that no man may judge him, that he must be forgiven, and, still more, may forgive himself. The mercy of "The Tree of Justice" does not contradict the justice of what has gone before. It keeps it sane.

The story tells how the Saxon king Harold survived Hastings and, having roamed the countryside as a half-crazed beggar for forty years, reappeared briefly just before his death, early in the reign of Henry I. Kipling does not picture Harold as sympathetic nationalist historians of the nineteenth century, such as J. R. Green, regarded him—that is, as a heroic champion of his people against a foreign invader. "The Tree of Justice" returns to a more authentic medieval conception. Harold was *faithless,* breaker of an oath of fealty sworn to William over holy relics at Rouen, and hence excommunicated. The oath may have been wrung from him. Nevertheless, the breaking of it was a crime in the eyes of his contemporaries:

> He caught me at Rouen—a lifetime ago. If I had not promised, I should have lain there all my life. What else could I have done? I have lain in a strait prison all my life none the less. There is no need to throw stones at me. (327–28)

What is suggested here is a mind cauterized by guilt, a man who sees his sufferings as inevitable and deserved. They are not even necessarily an expiation for the worst crime a medieval man could conceive.

Carefully, Kipling prepares the way for a possible act of forgiveness.

The poem that prefaces the story, "The Ballad of Minepit Shaw," reverses the opening moral statement of the book where, at the beginning of the collection, Thor's "cold iron," the burden of the moral law, duty and sacrifice, has been taken up. Here, in contrast, the poachers fleeing man's justice are told by "a man with a green lantern" to leave their iron crossbows behind—

> Oh, lay your crossbows on the bank
> And drop the knife from your hand,
> And though the hounds are at your flank
> I'll save you where you stand!
>
> (308)

They find themselves cast down Minepit Shaw, but miraculously are saved both from human judgment and from death.

The opening image of "The Tree of Justice" is one of cruelty; the tree itself carries the "poor little fluffy bodies" (311) of "vermin" the farmer has hung there. Once, though, "this sort of tree bore heavier fruit." The poor owls and stoats killed for hunting their necessary food are equated with the serfs hanged for killing their lord's deer. Justice, as men understand it, is fatally tainted, however necessary it may be, with expediency and cruelty. The first image strikes the chord that is to sound through the story until it dominates it at the end.

In the meantime, traces of the world in which the reader has moved until now persist. The Norman Sir Richard Dalyngridge and his Saxon friend Hugh, whom the children first met in *Puck of Pook's Hill*, have their "great burden" (314), the necessity "to make a fit, and above all, a safe sport," in the woodland for the king. This is because a Norman knight has been killed by a Saxon forester, and the king has decided he must demonstrate the security of his control over the conquered people by staging a great hunt. It was "his duty to show himself debonair to his English people" (314), and it was the duty of his lieges to see that he came to no harm. Richard's and Hugh's "work" was "to move the deer" into the area of the hunt, and then to control a population in a state of simmering resentment. The King Henry whom they serve is a tough and cynical politician who has usurped the throne from his incapable elder brother. Yet he is a sound administrator and a legal reformer, careful of the security of his realm and of "the Law" (326). Despite a tendency to cruelty, and the presence of timeservers and placemen like the bishop of Exeter, Henry represents, in an imperfect world, an order worth defending.

3 / *Rewards and Fairies:* Loyalty and Sacrifice

Harold, the by now legendary "traitor," is resurrected into this workaday world of power and politics. He is a tragic and enigmatic intruder who does not belong to schemes of civic order built on duty and labor. His suffering, guilt, and failure belong to different realms of being. "The Tree of Justice" forcibly juxtaposes these "two sides of the head." The king's jester Rahere, "a priest at heart" (325), forces the Norman courtiers, knights, and administrators to recognize the provisional, imperfect nature of the work they do and the lives they lead. They may be obliged to carry out their duties in a tarnished medium, since "one cannot build a house all of straight sticks" (330), but they can never be entitled to judge those who fail the tests of duty and sacrifice, like the fallen king whom Rahere has taken under his protection.

Rahere demands, "Lords of Man's Justice in your own bounds, do *you* mock my fool?" (333). He makes Henry and his officers see that they have been engaged in acts of policy that give them no moral superiority to Harold. This done, he is able to heal the guilt-crazed old man, who can die eased of his burden—"All the world's crazy chessboard neither mock nor judge thee" (334).

Hobden the countryman's rescue of the trapped dormouse, at the end of "The Tree of Justice," reinforces this assertion of the primacy of mercy over judgment. All that has gone before in *Rewards and Fairies* remains true. All the pattern of Thor's and Tyr's demands upon those who work to build or save society remains obligatory. Men are only men, however, and it is not for them to judge another's breaking of the laws of duty and sacrifice.

The enormous popularity of *Rewards and Fairies* and its role in the education of middle-class children, especially, are of considerable cultural significance. To understand it is to understand important aspects of their structure of feeling and of their moral response to their own and later times. The book is rooted in a specific historical climate where "duty" and "sacrifice" were widespread educational slogans. It has, besides, an unmistakable link with the largely forgotten ideals and social analyses of the Edwardian Tory Right, addressing itself to what it thought was a national crisis. Above all, however, *Rewards and Fairies* illustrates the power of art and imagination to transcend their context. These stories infuse the local and temporary catchphrases of an era and a faction with the vision and wisdom that can appeal to readers of other times and of opposing views.

4
Religious Crosscurrents in "The House Surgeon"

The subtlety of "The House Surgeon" (in *Actions and Reactions,* 1909) is chiefly found in its act of moral discrimination. It involves the posing against each other of two ways of life or ethical frames of reference, rendered not as sets of precepts but given body and color by an art of suggestive hints and indications. The tale begins on the evening after Easter Day with half-a-dozen men telling each other ghost stories. L. Maxwell M'leod Esq., playing patience by himself in the next alcove, overhears something about a curse on a family's firstborn, and leans across to inquire after the party has broken up. This opening, superficially resembling countless ghost stories of the period, has all the subtlety of Kipling's mature writing. There is the allusion to the central event of the Christian calendar, the Resurrection, the overwhelming affirmation of the Christian God's power over the world. The curse on the firstborn suggests the ultimate plague of Egypt that broke Pharaoh's will and redeemed Israel from the house of bondage. Easter and Passover are both offset, however, by curious and piquant intimations of the secular spirit. The evening after Easter is a time not for religion but for peasant superstition, ghost stories, only fragments of the supernatural. And the curse on the firstborn "turned out to be drains" (Kipling 1909, 263).

The effect of these allusions is to raise some slight crosscurrents at the very beginning of "The House Surgeon." There is a contrast between the great supernatural affirmations of the past—both essentially answers to evil, and redemptive in character—and the spirit of the present, the world of club raconteurs and the merely technical problems of drainage and plumbing.

"Maxwell M'leod" is very much part of this modern age. His assumed name carries a little of the pathos of the Jew at a time when assimilation seemed the answer to anti-Semitism. "Why didn't you join our party?"

4 / Religious Crosscurrents in "The House Surgeon"

(263), the narrator asks him, but the question remains unanswered. In private conversation "M'leod" reveals a gentle and sympathetic character. He takes a natural pleasure in his wealth and his power to obtain life's good things. There is a hint of naive boasting about his expenses and of naive puzzlement at their failure to secure a happy home for his family. Kipling compresses into a characteristic tone and gesture the shyness, the simplicity, the love of creature comfort, the touch of worldly cunning:

> "A man and his family ought to be happy after so much expense, ain't it?"
> He looked at me through the bottom of his glass. (264)

"M'leod" is a man interested in creating an atmosphere without pain or suffering. His insistence, at his wife's behest, that the house should have had no death in it since it was built is symptomatic. (The fact that a woman has accidentally fallen to her death just outside one of the windows is a joke at his expense as well as, for a different reason, at that of Homescroft's former owners.)

"M'leod" has pathos and charm, but unlike the "Jews in Shushan" of *Life's Handicap* he does not have tragedy. Despite their isolation as a tiny pocket in a remote Indian city, they had not lost touch with the passions of the Old Testament. The narrator there glimpses the apparently mild Ephraim slaughtering a sheep and marking the lintel of his door with its blood:

> He was attired in a strange raiment, having no relation to duster coats or list slippers . . . and the nature of the man seemed changed. . . . A picture of Ephraim busied in one of his religious capacities was no thing to be desired twice. (Kipling 1982, 293–94)

"M'leod" has lost touch with these roots of faith and suffering. His marriage to a Greek woman seems to signify his severance from his own people. He and his "good lady" live a sweet-tempered, indulgent life with their "little girl." ("I say little; but she's twenty" [264].) After having given thirty years of his life to the fur trade, he can only describe the depression to which the inmates of Holmescroft succumb as an auctioneer would, as something that "must be seen to be appreciated" (265) or as an illness, "an influenza epidemic," rather than in moral, spiritual, or even psychological terms.

The coziness, the comfort, the ebullient hospitality, and love of the good life are delicately handled by Kipling. There is nothing gross about

"M'leod," no trace of an anti-Semitic stereotype. The nub of the matter lies rather in his creation of a way of life that excludes tragedy, fatality, and mystery. Although some of his personal characteristics are necessary for the plot, one cannot help feeling that Kipling has noted a climate current in Judaism from Moses Mendelssohn in the eighteenth century to his own contemporary, the widely respected Israel Zangwill (Brown 1962, 556–62): the tendency to seek escape from the historical dilemma of the Jew through "assimilation" and the values of the Enlightenment. Liberal Judaism of this kind was dominant in Jewish circles when "The House Surgeon" was written.

"M'leod" is a charming exemplar of these values in their material rather than consciously intellectual sense. His "little place," Holmescroft, is an attractive suburban house in a new and "exclusive residential district of dustless roads" (266). The copper beech in the garden is "promising." He remarks on the cost of the building land and of the faintly absurd Queen Anne golfing pavilion. The house itself is lavishly furnished but close, the bedrooms smelling of perfumed soap. The antiseptic newness of everything seems designed to banish depth and the past. The many casual callers, including the "appropriately clothed" young men and maidens who play tennis, are pleasant but unmemorable.

> I was introduced to many fine ladies and gentlemen of those parts. Magnificently appointed landaus and covered motors swept in and out of the drive, and the air was gay with the merry outcries of the tennis players. As twilight drew on they all went away. . . . (269)

Darkness has been pushed to one side rather than dispelled. "M'leod" needs confirmation from the narrator. It is possible to flood Holmescroft with electric light from a switch in the veranda: "You can do that from your room also. . . . There's something in money, ain't it?" (270).

A house without darkness and where no death has ever taken place ought to still apprehensions they attempt to suppress. Miss M'leod hints at the possibility of the supernatural but associates it with Greece when she was a little girl, not England.

"The House Surgeon," however, is concerned not with the supernatural but with that element of the moral life the "M'leods" have tried to deny. The depression that comes on occupants of Holmescroft is not a fear of the unknown. In descriptions of it its palpability is emphasized. It is like a falling wall, the headlamp of a motor, a shining light, a black beam, a raging toothache, a burning glass. It produces physical symptoms, a click in the brain like the click in the ear of a man descending in a diving bell. The concrete imagery carries an association of something real and present, almost homely, rather than mysterious. One is amazed and angry at it rather than afraid. In comparing the feeling to the horror of great darkness mentioned in the Bible, Kipling implies that this very concrete thing is part of man's traditional knowledge and moral experience, something "M'leod's" ancestors knew but which he has forgotten. Its essence lies in the pain of conscience. We know of Evil because we have done evil. The narrator falls asleep and dreams "that most terrible of all dreams" in which all our misdeeds are wiped away, "and in the very bliss of our assured innocence, before our loves shriek and change countenance, we wake to the day we have earned" (273).

There are two inferences here. Human beings hurt those they love and they inevitably color their mental landscapes by their action. This is what the moneyed innocence of the "M'leods" ignores.

In this humane story, Kipling is not concerned to score a facile moralistic point about "M'leod's" way of life. What he does imply is that this charming, ingenuous man ignores the reality of "sin" and "guilt" in experience. As the narrator leaves after his second visit "M'leod" tries to console him with the gift of a narwhal horn from his collection, "much as a nurse gives a child sweets for being brave at the dentist's" (282). The moral dimension has been replaced by presents and gentle cajolery. Guilt has shrunk to embarrassment.

The moral sophistication of "The House Surgeon" is not content with making one fairly obvious statement about modern materialism or blandness. Whatever the previous inhabitants of Holmescroft, the Misses Moultrie, ignored, it was not the fact of sin. The "M'leods" may have forgotten it. By contrast the Misses Moultrie were soaked in it and Kipling does not suggest that their Calvinism is a superior wisdom. (After his childhood experiences this would scarcely have been likely.) Their religion is a festering and claustrophobic obsession, associated with a neurasthenic range of ailments that afflict the two sisters. The air of the sickroom conditions their lives in a world of "washes, gargles, pastilles and inhalations" (285), of secret devotion to rival medicines. The sisters share "a double-bedded room reeking with steam and Friar's Balsam" (285).

Their emotional range confines itself to narrow religious beliefs. The solicitor suggests that Miss Mary's brooding "along certain lines" in religion may have disturbed her mind. There is certainly something unhealthy in her almost automatic assumption that her sister's death was suicide and she seems to hug the thought of her eternal damnation:

> I warn you we are Evangelicals. We don't believe in prayers for the dead.
> "As the tree falls . . ." (292)

Kipling indicates that the obsession with sin, like "M'leod's" blandness, is a spiritual problem. Mary's Calvinism is presumptuous in its attempt to prescribe God's courses of action, to penetrate his mysteries. As Baxter remarks: "The facts as God knows 'em may be different—even after the most clinching evidence" (279).

The madness of her faith and the emotional intensity of her sheltered life are the fuel for a psychological "projection." The gloom of Holmescroft is the effect of her rigid moods and years of self-inflicted misery.

This "phantom of the living," an idea fashionable at the time, is less interesting than the role of the "house surgeon" himself. There is, in the title of the tale, a declaration of its medical dimension. The narrator is a kind of doctor, although the disease to which he ministers is spiritual and moral. His approach is calm and rational; he is seeking to apprise himself of the facts, pursuing various lines of inquiry in his diagnosis. Part of the pleasure of "The House Surgeon" probably stems, as Angus Wilson has suggested (1977, 238), from its sustained allusion to Sherlock Holmes and the detective work necessary before the source of the blight can be revealed. Without denying this particular nuance, however, it is probably worth emphasizing that the role of surgeon rather than detective is the dominant one. The narrator does more than unearth the salient facts. He ministers to a mind diseased and redresses a moral balance.

Kipling is careful to establish the narrator's attitude, his particular ambience. It is a blend of detachment, sympathy, tact, and humor, appropriate to the best kind of medical man. And this is surely significant. The problems are moral and spiritual. The solutions are the product of a medical analysis. The story affirms the value of calm deliberation and the power of sane human reason to cope. It is true that not just facts but questions of moral judgment are involved. There is an underlying optimism in the value given to evidence, however. If it is rationally assessed and forcibly presented, it will be effective. The narrator supplies proof that Mary's sister fell to her death accidentally and that proof is accepted. There is no suicide and therefore no eternal damnation. The depression over the house lifts.

4 / Religious Crosscurrents in "The House Surgeon"

Despite its praise of sanity and its basic optimism, "The House Surgeon" is not facile. Its point is that the dark moral places in life must be faced. The "M'leods" have not faced them. Miss M'leod calls the narrator "Mr. Perseus" and suggests that she will be chained to her rock unless he can save her (282). The allusion is apt. Perseus dealt with the horror of Medusa, not directly, but by catching her reflection in his shield. Human reason, through art and moral reflection, has power over fears, morbidity, and obsession.

The conclusion of "The House Surgeon" has all the subtlety and ambivalence associated with Kipling's middle and late phases. In one way, the story ultimately endorses the "M'leods'" values. When the evil has been faced and exorcised, their love of life, domestic happiness, and humanity are left free and, we are to feel, this is right. Miss M'leod's little song, the seeming end of the tale, is an affirmation of innocent joy as the best reaction to life. It rejects Calvinism and its angry God and implies that acceptance of one's limitations is the sanest response.

> Why should'st thou now unpleasant be
> Thy wrath against God venting
> That He a little bird made thee
> Thy silly head tormenting?
>
> (299)

The happiness of the "M'leods," the little birds, is not foolish. The contentment of God's humble children is, on the whole, fittest for their humanity, rather than a meddling with perplexity and mystery.

This is not the true end of "The House Surgeon," however. As in most of Kipling's later work, the story is not complete in itself. Its meaning is modified by the poem that accompanies it, the curiously named "Rabbi's Song." The theme of these verses, the power of thought to color "wall or beam or rafter" with its own unhappiness, is obviously pertinent to "The House Surgeon." More interestingly, the verses are a verdict on human life. The title of the poem possibly alludes to the "M'leods" but will perhaps recall to many readers Browning's "Rabbi Ben Ezra." Kipling sets against the classic statement of Liberal Judaism—"the best is yet to be," the view of another kind of rabbi, a hint of the earlier wisdom the "M'leods" had set aside:

> If Thought can reach to Heaven
> On Heaven it dwell

> For Fear that Thought be given
> Like power to reach to Hell.
>
> (301)

The power of thought means that it must be disciplined. Given the nature of things, escapes from the dark places are bound to be pieces of luck, or to depend, as they do in the story, on the intervention of a sane, reasonable, and sensitive man who is capable of facing the moral problem. He must protect those who are not capable of facing it and guard their peace for them. This is the "means" the poem refers to:

> Our lives, our tears, as water
> Are poured upon the ground;
> God giveth no man quarter,
> Yet God a means hath found;
> Though faith and hope have vanished
> And even love grows dim,
> A means whereby His banished
> Be not expelled from Him!
>
> (301)

5
The Redemption Theme in *Limits and Renewals*

"The Manner of Men" is an unusual story, a somewhat unexpected and intriguing variant on those themes prevalent in Kipling's late collection *Limits and Renewals*. Although it raises topics and deals with areas of interest found throughout the collection, it deals with them in a way radically different from the other stories, one that suggests a considerable effort of moral and imaginative sympathy. That Kipling should write well of types of feeling, of kinds of loyalty or intellectual predilections, that he *shared* is scarcely surprising. "The Manner of Men," however, is, among other things, an exploration of a sensibility to which Kipling was not naturally attracted, an intellectual climate for which he felt no instinctive liking. It was a mark of moral as well as intellectual distinction to write well, and with justice, about a cast of mind that he did not share. This was especially so when he wrote of what was emotionally unattractive and subversive of codes of behavior he endorsed and intellectual currents he thought valuable and timely.

It is, of course, no secret that *Limits and Renewals* offers several aspects of a subject variously called "healing," "forgiveness," "renewal," or "redemption." Much has been made of the sophistication of these stories, of their skillful omissions and weight of inferential material, and especially of a current of gentle humanity in them. Together with other stories of the later period, they provide a ready answer to accusations of crudity or cruelty made by critics of Kipling who have not read them.

Without denying the stories this value and importance, it is possible to see most of them as a continuation and development of interests and sympathies shown earlier. The attitude to healing and redemption has greatly gained in poignance and urgency because of the effect of 1914–18 on the individual mind and on a whole civilization. But the technique of healing is basically one in which Kipling had long been interested, as "The House Surgeon" suggests. He had long been evolving the codes and standards that dominate this late collection.

Two elements are emphasized in the acts of redemption studied in *Limits and Renewals:* the power of the rational mind working to uncover the source of guilt, fear, or neurosis, and esprit de corps.

The latter is nothing new in Kipling's work. Nor is the fact, often remarked on, that it is not exclusively or even predominantly military. Here, however, it is bound up, in interesting and suggestive ways, with acts of research into the past, probing to discover and exorcise some secret or some trauma. It has other implications as well. There are suggestions here that the esprit de corps is that of a band of researchers, enlightened sensitive men who confront the darkness. Their confidence rests on more than rationality, on more even than the comradeship of those who have learned and suffered together. It reposes ultimately on a simple, almost forgotten truth from which the techniques flow, a truth that underlies the attitudes and responses of the healers. Beyond their other bonds is one of shared knowledge. They possess an important secret, a clue to health and sanity in a dark, disordered world.

Kipling comes nearest to an explicit statement of what the secret is in the poem "The Threshold," which follows the story "Unprofessional." The "threshold" in the poem is that of the knowledge, now on the verge of rediscovery, that was possessed by the pre-Socratic philosophers but was strangled at its birth. Briefly, "The Threshold" offers a sketch of man's intellectual development. Men in their caves pictured the gods in an attempt to control and propitiate them by "sympathetic magic"—

> *In their deepest caverns of limestone*
> *They pictured the Gods of Food—*
> *The Horse, the Elk, and the Bison*
> *That the hunting might be good;*
> *With the Gods of Death and Terror—*
> *The Mammoth, Tiger, and Bear,*
> *And the pictures moved in the torchlight*
> *To show that the gods were there!*
>
> (Kipling 1932, 283)

For all their hold upon the imagination, these were the phantasms of a self-induced fear. The darkness was broken, briefly, by

5 / The Redemption Theme in *Limits and Renewals*

> *Crystal-eyed Sages of Ionia*
> *Who said, "These tales are lies..."*

These philosophers, the poem suggests, rejected a multiplicity of powers, gods and demons—

> *But each to be wooed by worship*
> *And won by sacrifice.*

On the contrary, all things were one substance, animated and differentiated by "one Breath." The universe is "one Matter," "Eternal, changeless, unseen," and above all "single" until "The Breath shalt bid it bring forth" into existence the forms that we perceive.

Although no philosopher, Kipling gives a sense of the *emotional* appeal of a teaching that has undoubted parallels in the views of Thales or Heraclitus (both of the Ionian school). Its principal attraction is a freeing from fear. Although Ionia is "Holy," the poem's emphasis is on gnosis, on a salvation to be obtained through knowledge, rather than through worship and sacrifice.

The arbitrary and mysterious are dispelled after the perception of an essential unity in the material world and in the spirit that animates it. Although complex in its manifestations, life may be grasped by the intellect. However elaborate, it is a pattern, not an enigma. Once the connections are perceived, the oneness of spirit and oneness of matter open ways in which ills of body and mind may be cured.

"Truth," the poem declared, "died at the Gate of Knowledge," on the verge of fruition, stifled by "anxious priests and wizards," the mystagogues of Egypt and Babylon, who "re-blinded the wakening land" and offered the shadows of superstition in place of the substance of understanding. "The Threshold" concludes by suggesting that, nevertheless, the aspirations of Ionia are once more about to be fulfilled.

The multiplicity of Kipling's imaginative reconstructions, and his sheer success in entering into so many minds and worlds, cautions the reader from too prompt an identification of the writer with any single statement he makes. Despite this necessary caution, in the context of *Limits and Renewals* "The Threshold" carries an unusual conviction.

It relates, most directly, to the story "Unprofessional," which it follows, but its spirit is found in various degrees in the other tales in the collection. There is a direction in them, a prevailing tendency of sane investigation and a comradeship in shedding light in dark corners.

"Unprofessional" is a study of a theory of synchronicity, of the notion of the connection of the material world with "tides" or rhythms, in what is a unitary and homogeneous cosmos. Although once dimly suggested in astrology, these rhythms are in no way occult. As Harries, one of the close-knit group of ex-soldier investigators, remarks, "They mean keeping one's eyes open and—logging the exact times that things happen" (257).

Minute observation will reveal, eventually, "on what system this dam' dynamo of our universe is wound" (257), disentangling the main rhythm from chance variations. Medical research has been "hung up" by "this rigid thinking game," enmeshed in its own techniques and preconceptions. But this sterility may be remedied by the single imperative, "Watch." If the right approach is made by fresh and unprejudiced and, above all, sharp-eyed observers, some clue will be found. Arduous, at times boring, though the routine work of observation and correlation may be, success is certain, given the certain existence of a humanly comprehensible pattern. To the question,

> "What do you suppose is the good of Research?"
> "God knows," Loftie replied. . . . "Only—only it looks sometimes—as if He were going to tell."
> "That's all we want," Harries coaxed. "Keep your eye on Him, and if He seems inclined to split about anything, put it down." (258)

This little exchange suggests one of the most attractive features of the story. Along with the feel for the intellectual endeavor of the research and a relish for the diverting ingenuity with which the researchers overcome obstacles and sidestep the "fated" death of their patient, "Unprofessional" evokes the bond between the healers themselves. It is a friendship "tried and proved beneath glaring and hostile moons in No Man's Land" (255). Their shared experience of war has stripped them "to the Ultimate Atom" before each other "pretty often" (256). They need no camouflage. The warmth of the relationship is conveyed by their freedom over money, their use of nicknames for each other, their seclusion in the converted school "in a suburb without too many trams" (26)—the site of their inquiries and experiments.

The secret of the rhythms or "tides" lies in determining the moment when cancerous tissue in a woman is most likely to be successfully operable. The operation succeeds and Mrs. Berners, their housekeeper, is saved. The pull of the grave, the disposition to suicide that follows her escape

5 / The Redemption Theme in *Limits and Renewals*

from her "fated end," is cheated in her case by a circumstantial accusation of dishonesty. Her indignation at the outrageous injustice of this diverts her mind from its death wish in a wildly funny scene (278–80).

The underlying "optimism" of "Unprofessional" requires little emphasis. Death itself may be only a phenomenon local to our planet. Deeper tides may run, "external to this swab of culture we call our world" (275). There are, however, other causes of suffering, at the "threshold" of which the story ends, half-wistful, half-resolute, that are darker than death.

One of the ex-officers-*cum*-scientists, Loftie, had married the "unstable" daughter of one of his earlier landladies. It is a source of an obscurely hinted but intense distress. When Frost—their "valet-plumber," the "ex-captain of a turret" (262) who plans to marry Mrs. Berners, learns that her operation will prevent her having children, he turns to Loftie. Both have had their "knock" (282), an experience of alcoholism and mental illness in their wives, since Frost's first wife had "disgraced" (282) him and died in an asylum.

The final vignette of the story somehow expresses its essential tone and values. It ends with the two men shaking hands, in their shared memory of grief, and Loftie's sympathy at the news he has to give. Frost's reaction is a curious half-expressed refusal to despair: "Pity! There ought to be some way of pulling 'em through it—somehow—oughtn't there?" (282). A handshake, and the tentative affirmation of power through knowledge, comradeship, and enlightenment are what the final image is intended to leave on the mind. And then follows, in an appropriately named poem, an evocation of a lost wisdom, cherished by a few and about to reemerge.

The *explicitly* Masonic element in Kipling's later work is not apt to be specially interesting, even if it is entirely comprehensible, to the non-Freemason. Nevertheless, it is possible to recognize the nature of its appeal to a part of Kipling's mind from a story such as "Unprofessional," which is colored by kindred ideals.

There is the coherence and consistency of a prevailing religious attitude in *Limits and Renewals*. It is an ideal to which those of Freemasonry, as commonly understood, are the best-known approximation in the real world. Needless to say, they are not ignoble or unsympathetic ideals either in life or as Kipling presents them in fiction. It is simply that, like any definite programme, they exclude as well as encompass.

It is the sharp awareness of what they exclude, of what spirit wars against them, which makes "The Manner of Men" so interesting in the contexts of *Limits and Renewals*. It is the odd man out in a collection dominated by the ideals of comradeship, and enlightenment of the *corps d'élite* finding salvation through knowledge for themselves and others.

Of course, this ideal is not as fully and openly stated in all the stories as it is in "Unprofessional." Elsewhere it is implied or understood, rather than developed at length. Its submerged presence is most easily seen in the way in which acts of healing involve the discovery of a secret, and the use of some fairly simple thing from the physical world, to conjure and control the psychological forces and to bring them back into their true courses. Renewal depends on *knowing,* and on utilizing the interaction of body and mind. The knowledge is predominantly the preserve of "officers," of men in some kind of "male bond," to use a handy piece of sociologists' jargon.

In the overtly Masonic tale "Fairy-kist," the opposition of knowledge to superstition, the unraveling of mystery through the rational inquiring minds of the masculine group, working in warm accord, again informs the atmosphere. What is interesting, incidentally, about the "Fraternity for the Perpetuation of Gratitude towards Lesser Lights," virtually a lodge, is an underlying religious attitude, noted early in the story. Bon vivants, old friends in an atmosphere of comfort and ease, very much men of the world, they are also gatherers of wisdom. This wisdom is available from many sources, even the humble Lesser Lights the society celebrates, and its teaching gives a calm assurance about the nature of life and death. The passage from one to another is natural and without mystery.

> "Corpses are foul things," Lemming mused aloud. "I wonder what sort of a corpse I shall make."
>
> "You'll never know," the gentle, silver-haired Burges replied.
>
> "You won't even know you're dead till you look in the glass and see no reflection. An old woman told me that once at Barnet Horse Fair—and I can't have been more than seven at the time."
>
> We were quiet for a few minutes, while the altar of the Lesser Lights, which is also our cigar-lighter, came into use. (154)

This passage evokes the ambience, as well as the aims of the brotherhood of truth-seekers. Intellectually, the act of gnosis grants freedom from fear. There is nothing dreadful and unknown, or at least nothing unknowable. The transition between life and death is easy because the universe is one, homogeneous.

The truth, like other truths, has a thousand humble witnesses, the Lesser Lights, who testify to its naturalness, its universality, the way in which it accommodates itself to the intellect. Whenever it is heard it is remembered. Somehow the altar-flame cigar lighter adds just the right touch, implying an easy movement between reverence for gifts and the familiarity of the fraternal group with its shared comforts. The truth may be precious, but those who recognize it can afford to relax in the certainty of their knowledge.

Nominally "Fairy-kist" tells of the solution of a murder mystery, but the moral weight of the story falls mainly on its act of illumination, the lifting of superstitious fear, of the sense of fatality and dread of mental illness. It is a revelation of the rationality of things. Skillfully, the narrator suggests the way in which suspicion focuses on Henry Wollin. His physical appearance ("wide as a bull between the eyes—no beauty" [161]), his evidently having been "a very sick man," and above all, the sheer persuasiveness of his West Country housekeeper whose quaint suggestions, in attempting to defend him, that he had been "kissed by the fairies" (164), driven "off his head" as a result of his war experiences, confirm Keede's own medical views:

> She had one of those slow, hypnotic voices, like cream from a jug. Everything she said squared with my own theories up to date. Wollin was on the break of life, and, given wounds, gas, and gangrene just at that crisis, why anything—Jack the Ripperism or religious mania—might come uppermost. (164–65)

Superstition and science seem to meet and support each other in condemning or condoning Wollin. Both are wide of the mark. The girl Ellen's death was caused, in fact, by a glancing blow from a girder in a badly loaded contractor's lorry. Wollin's presence shortly after with the apparent murder weapon, a fern trowel, is indeed due to a compulsion. This is not an urge to kill people but to plant flowers about the countryside "for such as had no gardens" (176). His obsession is the result not of mental illness, his own fancies, or some fatality, but of the effects of gas, coupled with a nurse's reading to him, while he was half-delirious, from *Mary's Meadows,* a children's book by Juliana Horatia Ewing.

The point about these bizarre explanations is their rationality. There are no demons, whether of fairyland or modern science. There is a plan, not necessarily accommodated to the narrator's preconceptions, but present nevertheless.

One curious element in this scheme is the value placed on gardening. McKnight, one of the investigators, is, like Wollin, a passionate gardener, and recognizes on the suspect's wall four prints of the "apostolic succession" of "the Four Great British Botanists" (178). For him, the book *Mary's Meadow* has a deep personal significance, containing, like the Gypsy woman's words on death, some deep hidden meaning:

> "The best, the kindest, the sweetest, the most eenocent tale ever the soul of woman gied birth to. I may sell tapioca for a living in the suburbs, but I know *that* . . ."
>
> He pulled the draw-chains of all the nine burners round the Altar of the Lesser Lights before we had a time to put it to the vote. (178)

Juliana Horatia Ewing's story is evidently a part of the corpus of traditions known to the few. What is being stressed seems to be the value of arcane knowledge handed down within a small circle.

As in "Unprofessional," there is a definite and coherent religious framework, the same emphasis on *intellectual* roads to salvation. Indeed, here the point is reinforced, since, as well as knowledge being rewarded, ignorance is punished. The information that saves Wollin's sanity destroys that of Jimmy Tigner, Ellen's last boyfriend. He is a "believing soul" (156) who lives with his mother, but simplicity of that kind has no value in the tale's scheme of things.

The bond of comradeship, also, is as central in "Fairy-kist" as elsewhere in the collection. The investigation, like the research in "Unprofessional," must be teamwork: "Most men and nearly all women commit murder single-handed; but no man likes to go man-hunting alone" (160).

It is perhaps unnecessary to show in detail that these are the values of the other stories in the collection that deal with redemption, such as "The Woman in His Life," "The Miracle of Saint Jubanus," and above all "The Tender Achilles." These have certain obvious points of similarity. In each case incipient mental disturbance is averted by a simple physical expedient.

In the first, a real dog, as a pet, is used to exorcise a phantom dog haunting a shell-shocked ex-soldier, now an overworked businessman. The dog causes him, in rescuing it, to relive and work out the underground horrors that caused his obsessions.

In the second, a young ex-soldier, "blasted, withered, dumb," toys endlessly with

> a little photograph—one of those accursed Kodak pictures, of a young man in a trench, dancing languorously with a skeleton. It was the nail of his obsession. . . . (327)

He is restored by a wilder dance—two acolytes and the village atheist caught upon the spokes of an umbrella, sliding and slithering about the floor of the church.

In the third, Wilkett suffers from hysterical guilt, brought on by overwork, at having through inefficiency caused the death of "a certain number of men" (356) in a wartime hospital for self-inflicted wounds. It is clear that guilt stems from obsessive perfectionism and morbid vanity. He is subjected to just such an operation as those he performed, is told that the diagnosis was a mistake, and, being obliged to relive the experience, sees it from another perspective.

In all these cases, as in "Unprofessional" and "Fairy-kist," there is an assumption of the close relationship between the psychological and spiritual. There is a belief that what is wrong is intellectually definable, and that it can be dispersed by an act of "sympathetic magic," a ritual reenactment of whatever originally caused it. The real problem is that of gaining correct information, but in each case a specific answer exists.

In suggesting the "philosophic schema" behind these acts of renewal, there is a risk of making them seem superficial. This is not the impression they make. In none of them is the fact of suffering, involving in each case nervous disorder or actual breakdown, glossed over or minimized. The problems are not easily solved, but they are *problems,* not a malaise or fate, and they are *solved,* not just endured. Throughout, it is the elite brotherhood of warm friends and coworkers who solve them.

Kipling's imagination seems gripped by what is, however relaxed and unpompous, a spiritual aristocracy. As presented, it is an attractive, intelligent, and humane ideal, but it represents a definite choice among spiritual values and approaches. *Gnosis,* while not incompatible with Christian *salvation,* does represent a very different emphasis in which contrition and humility in the theological sense (as distinct from good manners) have no necessary role to play.

In this connection it may seem odd to regard "The Manner of Men" as the challenging exception rather than the dark, mysterious, and deeply affecting "Dayspring Mishandled." So much has been and could be written about the latter that any suggestion about its meaning must be provisional. However, it does seem fairly clear that in all the hints, inferences, and weighted silences of the story there is one to which a special value should be given. One might almost venture to call it the "solution" of the tale, since it is the root of the matter. It is the precise moment when "dayspring" was "mishandled" for Castorley, and as a result for Manallace. As Castorley was dying "his pain broke through all the drugs," and a full, high, affected voice, unheard for a generation, accompanied, as it seemed, the clamour of a beast in agony, saying: "I wish to God someone would stop that old swine howling down there! I can't . . . I was going to tell you fellows that it would be a dam' long time before Graydon advanced *me* two quid." (31)

Deeper than the quest for power through scholarship, deeper than the element of sexual jealousy and revenge, at a lower level even than these in his personality, lies his sense of exclusion from the comradely bond. He recalls every detail from years before of the specific scene of his exclusion. What is suggested is that the exclusion may be antecedent to, and may even be the cause of, his deterioration. It is true he had "gifts of waking dislike" (5), but it is the early rejection by the syndicate that confirms and entrenches him in the prison of his isolation. Possibly he is despicable because he is despised.

In working with him on the forged Chaucer, Manallace establishes the relationship that had been refused earlier. However, the new bond is bizarre, convoluted, and secretly treacherous. Yet, once it is made, the victim becomes the "comrade," however deformed the connection, and it is impossible to destroy him.

In "Dayspring Mishandled" the two leading preoccupations of Kipling's philosophy of redemption—knowledge of the significant facts and the fraternal bond of coworkers—are essential to unraveling the problem of evil. It is a dark story, full of the feeling of how badly twisted a man's nature can become, but if the last revelation of the dying Castorley is the essential clue, even here the framework is rational. A solution is propounded. Redemption is possible through two connected means. One learns a secret, and one belongs to an exclusive group.

This slight sketch of Kipling's particular "religious" approach to the curative or regenerative theme in his later work is a useful context for the two roles in *Limits and Renewals* that explore the rise of Christianity. Significantly, both stories concentrate on the figure of St. Paul. Given the view of redemption and suffering found in the other stories, it is easy to see why Kipling should find Paul disturbing and, at times, repellent. Paul might be seen as the leading figure in the replacement of gnosis by sacrifice, salvation through knowledge by salvation through repentance, the exclusive group of educated initiates by the mass of humble believers, slaves, and women. A historical study of him remarks:

5 / The Redemption Theme in *Limits and Renewals*

What, in 1976, may seem the most fascinating and topical aspect of Paul is his recognition of *total change*. Not for him the easy assumption, prevalent in the Greco-Roman world, that all is a matter of historical traditions and background and age-old development. (Grant 1976, 197)

A process of learning could never really involve "total change" in the Pauline sense. Moreover, what Kipling seems to envisage in the other stories nowhere depends on a recognition of guilt or unworthiness. It is not primarily the filling of an emotional need, but the satisfaction of an intellectual search or the finding of the missing piece in the puzzle. The solution grows out of, or sustains, the arcane wisdom of the few.

Kipling's own emotional sympathies equipped him particularly well to understand those elements in the religious thought of the ancient world that Christianity combated and superseded, such as Gnosticism, the Mysteries, or the cult of Mithras. The worship of the god of light triumphant over darkness, the god of the brotherhood of soldiers, is one that, in intellect and feeling, Kipling could comprehend and recreate in *Puck of Pook's Hill* and in "The Church that was at Antioch."

The spirit that undermines the exclusive secret tradition reserved for the inner circle and attacks the ideal of a search for *enlightenment* rather than a giving up of heart and mind was bound to be as unsettling for Kipling as it was in the ancient world. The two Paul stories in *Limits and Renewals* touch on the leading features of the new faith's emotional and moral assault on religious disciplines and frameworks of the Mediterranean lands in the first century.

In "The Manner of Men" and "The Church that was at Antioch," Paul is examined as the prime enemy of tradition, of the inherited wisdom of the select group, and of the adjuncts of salvation through knowledge. Like Browning in the "Epistle of Karshish, the Arab Physician," Kipling is intrigued by what is an immense revolution in feeling rather than an intellectual discovery. Karshish has heard of men returning from the dead, but is disquieted by the intimation that "the All-Great" might be "the All-Loving too." Christianity, in Kipling's two Paul stories, is not the intellectual discovery of a secret. Valens in "The Church that was an Antioch" declares of the new sect that "There isn't a ceremony or symbol they haven't stolen from the Mithras ritual" (91).

Kipling emphasizes in his portrait the quality Michael Grant singles out in his study: "a massive urge to break down barriers between one human being and another" (Grant 1976, 196). Kipling represents Paul as a great spiritual popularizer, a broadcaster of what was always known but kept secret, as a man direct in his emotional appeals to everyone he meets, a breaker-down of reserves and reticences. All things to all men, he at once draws Valens out about route marches: "[A]nd, before he knew, Valens was reeling off his mileage on mountain-roads every step of which Paulus seemed to have trod" (Kipling 1932, 99).

A genius with a touch of vulgarity, Paul invades those private worlds, inner wheels, circles of the initiated brotherhoods, in which the elite seek enlightenment:

> He turned on Valens with a smile that half-captured the boy's heart. "Now—as a Roman and a Police officer—what think you of us Christians?" (100)

"Half-captured" is exactly right to express the combination of a powerful charm with the faint disquiet that Paul's directness and lack of inhibition and good taste provoke. He draws Valens out about the love of Mithras, leaving him "a little ashamed of having spoken of his faith" (101), and leaving his colleague Peter "dumb." Paul's style is characteristically imperative. He insists (101) and demands in a "hardish voice" (103) rather than "says." He speaks with an embarrassing freedom of his own religious conversion, buttonholing his hearers with "Listen a minute" (101).

Kipling's picture of Paul in "The Church that was at Antioch" is a delicately comic picture of the kind of man who would, or could, bring salvation within the reach of the masses. It leaves no doubt of the nature of the change in sensibility and religious feeling that was overtaking the Greco-Roman world. Kipling's own attitude to it is ambivalent. Ethically and in abstract, Paul's teachings are not new. The kinship with the Mithraic arcana recognized by Valens is admitted by Paul himself. What is new is the violent emotional directness that Paul infuses into the teachings and his universalism of appeal.

In fact, there is more than a touch of admiration in Kipling's portrait of him. He is a force to be reckoned with. Far more articulate than the genuine mystic Peter, with his intellectual confusions and hesitancies, Paul will conquer the world for the new faith. It is only when, presumptuously, he proposes to baptize the dying Valens that he is rebuked by his fellow apostle.

Kipling states one side of his view of the phenomenon of Paul in "The Disciple," the poem that follows "The Church that was at Antioch." Here

5 / The Redemption Theme in *Limits and Renewals*

the verdict is unfavorable. The disciple—one such as Paul, presumably—is he who

> ... shall change the Charter,
> Who shall split the Trust
> Amplify distinctions,
> Rationalise the Claim,
> Preaching that the Master
> Would have done the same.
>
> (115)

The gravamen of the charge seems to be one of popularization, the opening out of secret wisdom and its accommodation to a "mass market." "Split the Trust" suggests divulging a tradition, or breaking a bond of fellowship. Yet from another angle, this must be the price of founding a religion for the world and not just for the elite.

In "The Manner of Men," it is exactly this other angle of vision on Paul that we get. The story is at pains to establish, first of all, the patterning of relationships, the ways of feeling, that he disrupts and throws into doubt. When it is recognized that these established modes are those in which Kipling feels most at home, then his imaginative magnanimity can be recognized. He is questioning what he loves.

The young Spanish captain arriving at Marseilles and the elderly hook-nosed Sidonian port inspector, Quabil, engage in a short altercation about the way the Spaniard's boat is loaded, the state of the cargo, and the lifting of the planking round the hatch. Both are trying to put each other down in a competitive banter based on knowledge of the craft of the sea. Irritated, the captain declares that Quabil is an outsider, a landsman squatting over his brazier. In fact, he is one of the race of outsiders, a Jew. Quabil's answer is simply to prove that he belongs to the inner group, with its inherited wisdom and skills: "As he lifted his hand the falling sleeve showed the broad gold armlet with the triple vertical gouges which is only worn by master mariners who have used all three seas—Middle, Western and Eastern" (227).

The sailors—Baeticus the Spaniard, Quabil the Phoenician, and Sulinor the Dacian (whom we meet next)—belong to an exclusive brotherhood, despising Jews, of course, but also their Roman masters, whose real power extends only to the shoreline and whose fleet is manned by foreigners. They share common experiences of sea dangers and imperial bureaucracy.

Most significantly, however, the brotherhood of sailors, like the Mithraic cult or the Masons, has teachings about life and death, contained in a "Wet Prayer" for those drowning, to reconcile them to "The bride bed of Death"—

> "With us of the River," Sulinor volunteered, "we say: 'I sleep; presently I row again.'"
> "Ah! At our end of the world we cry: 'Gods, judge me not as a God, but a man whom the Ocean has broken.'"
> Baeticus looked at Quabil, who answered, raising his cup: "We Sidonians say, 'Mother of Carthage, I return my oar!' But it all comes to one in the end." (239)

What is suggested here is a view of life fundamentally at one with that achieved by other elite groups of wisdom seekers in the later stories. Life and death form a homogeneous substance, a pattern contained and explained in the tradition, and a right passage through the pattern depends on knowledge. One draws confidence, and presumably peace of mind, from the disciplines of the inward-turned exclusive group. It may "all come to one in the end," but in this present life the particular rites and formulae dividing the elite from the generality are essential and must be preserved.

This is the view that St. Paul challenges in "The Manner of Men," as he did in the real first-century world. He shares with the Paul of "The Church that was at Antioch" an emotional directness and flexibility, partly attractive, at times slightly repellent:

> "And he was worth talking to, Red," said Sulinor.
> "You thought so; but he had the woman's trick of taking the tone and colour of whoever he talked to." (232)

In his time onboard ship with Sulinor and Quabil in the journey to Rome, Paul produces a different reaction in the two men. Quabil is overtly hostile, racially averse as a Sidonian to a Jew, suspicious of one whom he takes to be a magician, but keen-sighted enough to recognize that Paul is in some way emotionally a threat. The Phoenician's reserve and bitterness presumably stem, at least in part, from a further cause: the death of the son who resembled Baeticus, a year before the voyage with Paul, and of which the reader is only told at the end of the tale. This is a characteristically subtle late-Kipling narrative touch, reserving information that throws the material already presented into a different light.

The bereaved and fearful Quabil is in no condition to accept any kind of direct approach or appeal from Paul, a fact that the apostle tactfully recognizes

"When he saw that trying to—er—cheer me made me angry, he dropped it."
"Like a woman again." (238)

He turns instead to Sulinor, with whom he has long conversations about "Kings and Cities and Gods and Caesar." Quabil recognizes that there is a motive for these beyond simple friendliness—

"Hadn't you wit to see he never wanted you for yourself, but to get something out of you?" Quabil snapped. (238)

What Paul does get out of the Dacian ex-pirate is his terrible fear of "the beasts," of death in the arena, to which he is liable, a thought to which he many times reverts. In fact, Sulinor is on the run and anxious to avoid too close inquiry into his past. His fear of that particular death stems from a terrible childhood experience that has scarred him physically and mentally.

Kipling suggests that both Quabil and Sulinor have undertaken the perilous Mediterranean winter voyage, which was rarely made in the ancient world, nominally because of the good financial inducement from Caesar, but really to escape from private grief and private fear. Much of Kipling's art here, as elsewhere in his later work, lies in avoiding the explicit. What confirms this interpretation is Sulinor's confession that *rationally,* there was a chance of escape from the storm, but that their hope and confidence had simply (and presumably symptomatically) given out:

"We were doomed men all. You said it, Red."
"Only when I was at my emptiest. Otherwise I *knew* that with any luck I could have fetched Sicily! But I broke—we broke. Yes, we got ready—you too—for the Wet Prayer." (238)

In *The Myth of the Eternal Return,* Mircea Eliade has described the significance of Christianity in disrupting the cyclic conception of time conceived as a snake with its tail in its mouth, returning upon itself, a pattern prevalent in the ancient world. Instead, the new religion showed that things happen once and for all. Action is decisive, not determined or fated, and it is possible to make a new beginning. Perhaps against his natural sympathies,

Kipling's imagination seizes on the spirit of the unexpected disruptive force coming from outside and breaking up the cyclical, predetermined, patterned conceptions of life:

> He clawed his way up the ladders and said: "No need to call on what isn't there. My God sends me sure word that I shall see Caesar." (239)

The claim is impudent and outrageous, made by one who does not know the received wisdom of the enclosed group. It negates the traditional ritual. Perhaps Kipling means to imply, in Baeticus's comment on the chorus of Arlesian girls singing a ship out of Marseilles harbor ("And you'd think they meant it"), that these traditions are fatigued, have lost their inner meaning.

The miracle announced by the outsider happens, and not a life is lost. Paul confirms the moral as well as physical rescue of the two men by eating appropriately chosen food with each in turn—salt fish for the Semite, pork for the Gentile. He confirms to first one, then the other, his certainty of their eventual safety.

For Quabil and Sulinor the result of the shipwreck and complete destruction of the *Eirene* is not a prolongation of their old life but the creation of a new one. Quabil leaves the sea and becomes a port inspector at Marseilles, far away from Lebanon where his son was drowned. By the time he meets Baeticus his grief has faded enough for him to be able to speak freely of how the young Spaniard reminds him of the child he has lost.

Paul's effect on Sulinor is even more decisive. He advises him to avoid Caesar's law by becoming one of its instruments: "By taking service, you will be free from the fear that has ridden you all your life" (248). Revealed at the end of "The Manner of Men," Paul's ultimate attitude to the ritual formulae, the patterns of behavior, and group codes that his new message supersedes is subversive and unintentionally insulting:

> "You are not canvas I can cut to advantage at present. But if you serve Caesar you will be obeying at least some sort of law." He talked as though I were a barbarian. Weak as I was, I could have snapped his back with my bare hands. (248)

Paul is quite content to grant the code its use and work within it if this happens to be convenient, as he serves each man the appropriate food. In the end, however, his miraculous, seemingly irrational Evangel renders the past obsolete.

Kipling's story is a remarkable intuitive picture of a crisis in religious history, the movement from gnosis for the few to salvation for the many. He portrays an explosion that wrecked all established patterns within which men had found their place in this and other worlds and overturned traditional rites and rituals, such as those he elsewhere celebrated. The new message destroys all the expectations of appropriate behavior.

Sulinor, a little affected by the wine they are drinking, recalls Paul's extraordinary paradoxes. He is a "philosopher" who does not seek truth calmly, but in ordeals and suffering, a man going willingly to see Caesar on an important errand, who willingly performs a degrading office:

> "And he—he had washed me clean after dysentery!"
> "Mother of Carthage, you never told me that!" said Quabil.
> "Nor should I now, had the wine been weaker." (249)

Kipling's success in portraying the heroism and moral dignity of salvation through knowledge is matched by his success in capturing this very different and perhaps ultimately more powerful and mysterious new salvation. His success testifies to the magnanimity of his imagination.

6
The Limits of Knowledge: "The Eye of Allah"

Kipling's "The Eye of Allah," which was first published in the *Strand* magazine in 1920, before being collected in *Debits and Credits* in 1926, is generally regarded as sharing that peculiar density on which its author prided himself in the last phase of his writing. As J. M. S. Tompkins long ago pointed out, although its main theme is that of a scientific advance for which the world is not ready, the tale is "doing several things at once" (1965, 168). C. A. Bodelsen has usefully summarized the most obvious and significant of these layers of meaning or areas of concern. Most readers would presumably accept this:

> "The Eye of Allah" is on one level a story about what happens to a group of people in a medieval monastery; on another level it is a story about a premature discovery (the microscope); on a third it is about the impact of the Renaissance on the medieval world picture; on the fourth about the attitude of the artist, the physician, and the philosopher to science; and on the fifth about four aspects of civilisation personified as the artist, the scientist, the philosopher, and the Church dignitary and statesman, and illustrated by confronting them with an emblem of the new science: the microscope. (1964, 91–92)

If it is possible to set out a late Kipling story as a map or a diagram, then this provides a workable and sensible one for "The Eye of Allah." These, among several others, are undoubtedly directions in which a reader's eye might wander, some of those "overlaid tints and textures" offered, in Kipling's own often-quoted phrase, to the "shifting light of sex, youth and experience." More than one writer, too, has noted the likeness between the untimely discovery of the microscope in "The Eye of Allah" and the premature invention of the stethoscope in "Marklake Witches" (1910). Both stories, it has been plausibly suggested, are rooted in a religious sense that "man must fit himself to a given world" (Mason 1975, 256) and that our ignorance is a necessary veil between us and God.

However, in spite of such acknowledgments of the story's many levels and of the fundamental seriousness of a theme deeply ingrained in Kipling's conception of the facts of living, it is easy to feel one has missed some focus in which the several lines of meaning link together. What lies behind the intricate texture of the writing in "The Eye of Allah," its loaded silences, calculated lacunae, and the weight of its implications? A useful starting point is to consider the care with which a very specific date and ambience are established in the narrative and in which a number of historical references are unobtrusively placed, involving their own particular and intriguing implications. The trouble with Bodelsen's list and with others like it is that, although sensible enough, they direct the reader to general considerations ("a group of people in a medieval monastery," "a premature discovery," the "attitudes of the artist, the philosopher and the physician"), to wider themes that, although they do color the narrative, are refracted within it through the medium of the particular. The same might be said of "explanations" of the story in terms of Kipling's undoubted, but again *general,* sense of the need of a veil over reality, a sense that, as he remarked to Rider Haggard, "God does not mean we should get too near lest we become unfitted for our work in the world" (quoted in Mason 1975, 258). There is, after all, an enormous gulf between the atmosphere and import of "Marklake Witches" and that of "The Eye of Allah." The stethoscope in the former story was to have been discovered within a few years anyway, and the fact that it is not revealed to the world earlier has no public significance. The importance of the invention lies in the private but admittedly poignant reactions it sets off in the circle surrounding the dying girl, Philadelphia. By contrast, the abortive microscope of "The Eye of Allah" is the means to explore the quality of a whole civilization. The precise instant at which it is explored is of crucial importance in appreciating the full meaning of the story.

Lisa Lewis has convincingly pinpointed the supposed date of "The Eye of Allah" as 1266 or 1267 (Kipling 1987, 311). Cardinal Falcodi, mentioned at the beginning of the tale as papal legate in England, has been made pope when it ends. Kipling builds a number of allusions and suggestions around this precise dating that impart a specific quality to the story. They are much more than decoration and local color. However, in pointing them out or in dwelling on them, one might seem to run the risk of pedantry, or of reducing "The Eye of Allah" to a learned (or would-be learned) diversion, of preferring contextual minutiae to major themes. The point is, of course, that themes and context cannot here be separated.

The evidence of Kipling's own use of learned allusion and for the degree to which he intended it to be integral to his writing are somewhat contradictory, yet intriguing. Admittedly, he felt the danger of work "overloaded with verified references" that had as much "feeling" as "a walking stick." His "Daemon," he appreciated, would not "function in schoolrooms." Yet at the same time he prided himself on the "gamble" or "petty triumph" by which he might anticipate the findings of scholarship by force of imagination (Kipling 1990, 109–10). More to the purpose, his stated reason for ignoring reviewers of his work, after some initial personal encounters, was the "slenderness of some of those writers' equipment," their casual knowledge of French literature, as well as of "much English grounding that I had supposed indispensable" (123). In "The Eye of Allah" his "grounding" in early French literature provided him with the focal point for a consideration of the endangered consummation of a culture.

The story belongs to that late phase of his writing when he wished to produce work that was oblique, profound, and multilayered. If "Dayspring Mishandled" was, as critics have suggested, conceived as an "answer to the intellectuals" whom Kipling publicly affected to despise, and a display of that "difficulty" that they had begun to demand, as the modernist current gathered force in literature, then it would not be unreasonable to expect curious undercurrents and mixed motives, this time displayed through historical references, in "The Eye of Allah."

Two images must strike almost any reader as crucially important in establishing the story's cultural concerns. J. M. S. Tompkins has noticed the first of these: how in one of Kipling's "marvellous compressed sentences of landscape, atmosphere, period and symbol" (Tompkins 1965, 168), artist, scientist, physician, and abbot see "three English counties laid out in evening sunshine around them; church upon church, monastery upon monastery, cell after cell, and the bulk of a vast cathedral moored on the edge of the banked shoals of sunset" (Kipling 1926, 389–90). She identifies the "moored cathedral" as a "ship of war" that required the beauty and menace of the world around it to act as its principle of order.

Kipling's comments in *Something of Myself* help to illuminate the image still further. He describes his ruminations in his Villiers Street lodgings during the early stages of his career as a writer in London, and how his

6 / The Limits of Knowledge: "The Eye of Allah"

"original notion" of England's role in the "world outside England" developed. It grew into "a vast, vague conspectus" of the "whole sweep and meaning of things and effort and origins throughout the Empire. I visualized it, as I do most ideas, in the shape of a semi-circle of buildings and temples projecting into a sea—of dreams" (1990, 54–55). After visualizing the meaning of the empire in this manner, he felt he had "got it straight in his head" and that he had no more need to "knock" his readers "in the abstract." The similarity of the image to the one that, in "The Eye of Allah," embodies the medieval religious and social order is interesting. In each case a culture and a political order are embodied in buildings that suggest in concrete form their already existing man-made achievements. In each case the definite outline of a group of buildings has as its background the undefined, the inchoate, "a sea of dreams" or "a shoal of clouds." Kipling visualized "most ideas," and notably those about human societies, in a fashion that emphasized the contrast between known and unknown, formed and formless, the established concepts, values, or creeds and the indeterminate "dreams" that lay outside, perhaps threatening, but, in any case, necessarily excluded. He sensed that the image *told* more about the essential nature of a culture or a political entity than any "abstract" statement about its aims or features.

Kipling's account of how he overcame his "writer's block" over "The Eye of Allah" is interesting in this connection. After the story had again and again gone "dead under his hand" his "Daemon" prompted him: "'Treat it as an illuminated manuscript.' I had ridden off on hard black-and-white decoration, instead of pumicing the whole thing ivory-smooth and loading it with thick colour and gilt" (122). Although it is hard to tease out the implications of this somewhat cryptic observation, it seems to refer to more than the decorative surface of the tale. The "hard black-and-white" suggests a too precise or schematic presentation of the theme in the original version. The outline was too clear, the lines of meaning were too sharp. What he needed was an image, like that of the circle of buildings projecting into a sea of dreams that embodied the British Empire, by which the subtler implications of his idea might be conveyed without a trite explicitness. At first sight, it seems something of an anticlimax, after his heart-searching, for his "Daemon" to tell him that a medieval illumination would convey the atmosphere of the Middle Ages. His common sense might presumably have told him as much. The value and significance of the daemonic advice becomes clearer if one looks more closely at the second of the tale's key images, the description of the miniature of the Annunciation on which

John of Burgos is working when "The Eye of Allah" opens, and which, it is clear, Kipling has placed there to establish much of the mood and meaning of what is to follow. The "lattice of infinitely intricate arabesque" (366), the "sprays of orange bloom," the "blue hot air," and the "parched landscape" of the picture of the Virgin hearing the first words of the "Magnificat" represent an extraordinary fusion of sacred and secular, erotic and religious. John has deliberately substituted the sprays of orange bloom for the conventional flower in a vase representing spring, the time at which the Annunciation was first supposed to have taken place ("When absent it [the flower in a vase] is due to a slip of the artist's, for the arrangement of the scene was rigidly fixed" [Male 1958, 244]). The vivid and palpitating intensity of the miniature (its background, significantly, "red-lac" rather than the expected gold, the halo hardly yet "fired" rather than painted) is drawn in part obviously, from John's own memory of and yearning for the Jewish mistress he has left in Spain. It is the landscape "down south . . . Granada way" (Kipling 1926, 366) in which the Virgin sits. Yet, however unconventional in its detail, the picture, paradoxically, catches an essential feature of the medieval spiritual climate. John himself sees no contradiction between the passion he feels for the woman and the subsuming of that passion into a painting of the Virgin. To the subcantor's remark "You've made her all Jewess" (366), he replies "What else was Our Lady?" What John is asserting is that "equilibrium" or "harmony" that Emile Male's seminal study, the most influential and widely read account of the medieval vision in the years before "The Eye of Allah" was written, claimed for the art of the cathedrals: that "white light before its division by the prism into multiple rays" (Male 1958, 397). In that vision human nature, "disintegrated" by daily work and light, might renew its unity.

One phrase in Kipling's description, fraught with implication, catches that unity of feeling. The eyes of the figure in John of Burgos's miniature are "charged with foreknowledge" (366). That "foreknowledge" is, on one level, the Virgin's prevision of the suffering and death of the Son she is to bear; on another it is the foreboding of John's Jewish mistress about the future of their love, fear all too poignantly justified by coming events and which, as an artist, he has sensed. The union between human and divine love in that first glimpse of a medieval picture embodies something of that emotional unity which led St. Bernard to praise the Virgin in a *Commentary on the Song of Songs* in the language of a human love "incandescent in its fervour" (Heer 1963, 108) or which prompted Raymond Lull to clothe mysticism in erotic imagery in *The Book of the Lover and the Beloved*. It is a fact of the medieval vision, easy to parody or to coarsen, but abundantly proved by (and essential to an understanding of) its art and its religion.

"The Eye of Allah" insists, from the first, on another aspect of the unity of medieval culture and feeling that is almost equally significant. The monastery of St. Illod's is a world of ardent specialists. The cantor is too much a musician to concern himself with the library (Kipling 1926, 365). The subcantor who "idolized every detail of the work" (365) is the "masterfool of Christendie" outside the scriptorium (374). Brother Martin takes pride in his "really good page-work" (372). John of Burgos, "to whom men were but matter for drawings" (368), can hardly bear to "break off" work on his miniature. The infirmarian, Brother Thomas, is "meek but deadly persistent" (367) in the pursuit of drugs. The abbot, "a man of science above all" (367), whose heart is "more in the monastery's hospital work than its religious" (368), offers John in his bereavement the thought that "outside God's Grace" there is but "one drug; and that is a man's craft, learning, or other helpful motion of his own mind" (372). John agrees that this "coming to "him (372) will be his consolation but has, in any case, already replied to the abbot's lady's attempts at comfort that he has his art (371).

In one way, there is nothing in this emphasis on work, other instances of which might be quoted from "The Eye of Allah," which will surprise any reader of Kipling. C. S. Lewis's description of him as "first and foremost the poet of work (1969, 235), who reclaimed for literature the enormous area taken up by the earning of daily bread, has, rightly, become a truism of Kipling criticism, enshrining a basic and permanently useful perception about his writing. However, "The Eye of Allah" is significantly different from his numerous other celebrations of work in that it does not link that celebration with slavery to the "Inner Ring" (Lewis 1969, 248), the charmed circle or professional brotherhood sharing the exhilarations of comradeship, communal knowledge, or the code words of some skill—or mystery. Instead, the monastery of St. Illod's is a collegiate body with an atmosphere somewhat resembling the one a university was once ideally supposed to achieve, and sometimes did. It is a place in which individuals pursue their own studies to the highest point of perfection while regarding those of others with indifference or bemused toleration. Yet the monastery is still a body. The specialists live under a corporate discipline and their skills serve and glorify the religion that they share. From the first, "The Eye of Allah" is concerned with the imperiled but valuable balance between the appetites and enthusiasms of individuals and the claims of the community, as much as it is with the balance or unity between sacred and profane *within* the individual sensibility. The opening description of John's miniature suggests how the erotic and the devotional may link together and enhance each other. The tale's initial intimation about the scope and nature of authority within the monastery, and within the society that has produced it, point to the other link between specialisms, and a common culture. An unquestioned authority, precisely because it is unquestioned, is able to show great practical indulgence to those whom it rules. Abbot Stephen de Sautré is a "reasonable disciplinarian" (367), using his enormous power deftly and unassertively, without ever letting it slip but without crushing the private enthusiasms of those in his charge, until the denouement of "The Eye of Allah." It is because the lines are so firmly drawn in this world that corners may be cut. John of Burgos breaks the rule about attending Vespers while the subcantor only "waited patiently" (365). He has established a loose connection with St. Illod's to assist him during his journeys abroad, but the "claim was gladly allowed" because of his knowledge of the arts. The abbot permits his visit to his Spanish mistress and it is, at most, mildly deprecated by the "doubtful" (366) subcantor.

John is merely reminded that it would be a sensible "precaution," when going on a long journey, to obtain absolution for his existing sins before adding to them. It is a step as practical as that of recutting his tonsure to obtain clerical privilege and "consideration on the road" (367).

The abbot is no less indulgent to himself than to others in the matter of clerical celibacy and his "lady," Anne of Norton, enjoys a respected if low-key position in the monastery, as a wife in all but name. Stephen de Sautré demonstrates the permanent nature of his authority, and his readiness to relax it from time to time, in two striking formal gestures. Over dessert, after his "Wisdom Dinner," he draws off his abbatial ring, emblem of his office and rule, and drops it "that all might hear the tinkle, into an empty silver cup" (379). His role being understood and unchallenged, he may step outside it and allow his guests to speak freely. However, when Roger Bacon tried to keep the microscope, Stephen "leaned forward, fished his ring out of the cup, and slipped it on his finger" (391). The resumed authority cannot be resisted.

The text suggests that Stephen's "Wisdom Dinner," a formalized exchange of learning and opinion in pleasant surroundings, strikes the other monks as a little odd, an idiosyncrasy of the abbot ("one of his 'wisdom' dinners" [375]). They dress for it in academic costume but it is not a standard medieval *disputatio*. The nearest analogy for it is eastern, "those banquets of the learned" organized by contemporary Moslem rulers. Al Kamil (1218–38), for example, a little earlier than Stephen's captivity after Mansura, had "fifty scholars reclined on divans round his throne to provide his evening conversation" (Kantorowicz 1957, 108). The abbot's ritual granting of free speech through a formalized gesture is also eastern, recalling for instance, similar gestures by Harun Al Raschid in *The Arabian Nights* (Mardrus and Mathers 1958, 2:427, 4:146). Perhaps Stephen had seen the throwing of a ring into a cup during his captivity in Cairo.

The balances between the conflicting claims of freedom and authority, individual enthusiasm and communal life, sacred and secular, that "The Eye of Allah" suggests are peculiarly delicate. The story catches the very moment of poise in a civilization between germination and decay, when the circle of buildings, complete in its elaborate particulars, holds back the "sea of dreams." What the tale implies about such a moment is that it is one of peculiar value, when the ripest fruits appear and a culture gives of its best. Deftly, Kipling sketches in the spiritual, intellectual, and psychological implications of the textbook phrase, "the height of the Middle Ages."

The poem in *Debits and Credits* placed to follow the story ("The Last Ode," one of Kipling's imitations of Horace) offers an illuminating secondary comment on such a moment. The Horace of the poem cannot but be impressed by Virgil's messianic prophecy of "A Star new-risen above the living and the dead" and the dawn of a new age. Yet "The Last Ode" concludes touchingly on a note of doubt:

> Maecenas waits me on the Esquiline
> Thither tonight go I . . .
> And shall this dawn restore us, Virgil mine,
> To dawn? Beneath what sky?
>
> (Kipling 1987, 395)

Will the change at hand, with its new and perhaps necessary virtues, have room for men like Horace and his friend, types of a classical civilization at its ripest, most urbane, and tolerant but who, unlike the spiritual Virgil, had not "received the word"?

Kipling could have chosen no better date than 1266–67 for "The Eye of Allah" to catch such a ripe yet poignant moment of culmination. On a fairly simple level, of course, the choice of date enriches the story with contextual implications. To choose one example, Roger of Salerno is, in general terms, the traditional medieval figure of the medical man, indifferent or hostile to religion, a figure best known from Chaucer's Doctor of Physik. The text refers explicitly to this proverbial hostility of medicine to religion ("Three doctors—counting Stephen. I've always found that means two atheists" [376]). However, Roger has another dimension, suggested by his reference to the bishops of the Church who "strew our roads in Italy with carcasses they make for their pleasure or wrath" (380). His university of Salerno, "situated at the meeting place of Greek, Latin, Arabic and Jewish culture," had flourished through the generosity of the Hohenstaufen emperor Frederick II, who "came to its rescue" in 1231 (Tanner, Orton, and Brook 1927, 6:562). It was part of that brilliant, hybrid, half-secularized culture associated with Frederick, called the "Stupor Mundi" for his outrageous (to the medieval mind) views on religion. He was supposed to have attacked Moses, Christ, and Mahomet as "three deceivers" (Kantorowicz 1957, 500) and, almost equally shocking, preferred to end his "crusade" without striking a blow, in civilized discussion with Sultan Al Kamil (Runciman 1965, 3:187–90). From 1265 to 1268, the period of "The Eye of Allah," the papacy was winning its long duel, political and religious, against the Hohenstaufen. In 1266, one heir, Manfred, was killed at Benevento. In 1268, the other, the handsome youth Conradin, was executed at Naples. The ruthlessness of the Church in this feud aroused deep outrage, which echoes in Dante (*Purgatory,* canto 3), and which colors the embittered character of Roger of Salerno, as Kipling represents him. Roger is a man living through the crushing out of his world.

However, the dating and references in "The Eye of Allah" affect its meaning in far more than a purely contextual sense. Any reading of the story must attend closely to the character of Stephen de Sautré, the "lame, dark Abbot" (Kipling 1926, 367) who surprises John and the infirmarian Thomas, since he has "learned to walk softly" in his two-year captivity among the Saracens at Cairo. This experience, involving several complex and even contradictory strands, has shaped Stephen's mind and is the determining factor in his decision to destroy the microscope, the climactic incident of "The Eye of Allah."

One layer of Stephen's experience in Egypt was clearly erotic. It is implied that, as John was doing in Spain, he embarked on a love affair with an "infidel." After giving the artist his absolution, he asks what he is seeking on "this journey" (368). "Devils mostly," says John, grinning. The word "mostly," with its hint that there is something else, and the grin suggest the shared joke of men in the same predicament, supposedly celibate monks with mistresses. The unspoken jest continues in John's reply to the abbot's

6 / The Limits of Knowledge: "The Eye of Allah"

next question: "Are not Abana and Pharphar—?" (that is, can he not find what he is looking for at home, as Naaman the Syrian wished to do in 2 Kings 5–12?). The artist's response hints broadly at the double meaning of "devils" and at the two men's troubles over women. Since he is also "well-born," he can tease Stephen about his "lady." He looked "the Abbot full in the face and 'Did *you* find it so?' said he" (368). Since Stephen does not speak about the *intellectual* influences of his time in Cairo until near the very end of the story, the "devils" at this point seem to involve something else, buried in the shared joke about John's and the abbot's relations with women. John's boldness is about something he *knows*. But what are the "devils" that live beside the abbot's own Abana and Pharphar? What John seems to be referring to, when he looks Stephen full in the face, is the friction in the latter's relationship with his "lady," Anne of Norton. There is a strong implication that their relationship is an unhappy one, in spite of the abbot's love for the woman (confirmed in John's "God pity Stephen" [376] when he hears she is dying of cancer). Anne's strange choice of consolation for John, when she hears he has lost both the Jewish woman and his child, points more clearly to the sadness in her own love for de Sautré. She tells John to "remember there's no jealousy in the grave" (371). Presumably this is the feeling from which only death can relieve the "always ailing woman who followed the abbot with her sunk eyes." Who or what is it she is jealous of? There is no hint anywhere in the text of a contemporary English rival for the abbot's love. What is suggested, however, is the existence of an unlaid ghost from the past. This becomes as explicit as anything in Kipling's late narrative style when we are told that although the "Abbot had reason to recall, unions between Christian and Infidel led to sorrow" (370), as he sees John clatter off to Southampton on the way to Spain and his Jewish love, "Stephen envied him." A further hint is conveyed in Stephen's remark, made with a sigh, that John's love may be converted. Perhaps he recalls that this "hope" was a vain one in his case. It is fairly clear that the affair in Cairo, whatever its exact circumstances, somehow affected the later bond between Anne of Norton and de Sautré. This is what lies behind the abbot's advice to pursue his craft as the remedy for pain of the soul.

The peculiar unhappiness sometimes inherent in love across the lines of race or culture was a subject that interested Kipling. His best-known treatment is, of course, the poignant "Without Benefit of Clergy." In "The Eye of Allah," by contrast, the theme is undeveloped and implicit, providing an undercurrent rather than a complete explanation of Stephen de Sautré.

Much more, and far worse, happened to him in his captivity after Mansura than happened to John and the Jewish woman, or even to Holden and Ameera in "Without Benefit of Clergy."

Another line along which Kipling directs the reader's eye lies in Stephen's remark, after he has smashed the microscope with John's dagger's hilt, that "what you have seen, I saw long since among the physicians at Cairo. And I know what doctrine they drew from it" (393–94). What exactly is he referring to? His comment, with its suggestion of some kind of soulless or perverted science, does indeed offer a sufficient motivation, at a fairly superficial level, for his act of destruction. However, the cryptic allusion is, at the same time, one of the most important of the overlaid "tints and textures" in the story that are meant to sustain its different levels of meaning.

"The Eye of Allah" is set within the last years of Thomas Aquinas's life and at the culmination of his career, during which he was engaged on the *Summa Contra Gentiles* and the *Summa Theologica*. These great works of synthesis represent, among much else, answers to "the panic upon the Aristotelian peril, that had passed across the high places of the Church." (Chesterton 1956, 171). As is generally accepted, Aquinas was writing in response to the work of the great Moslem commentators on Aristotle, especially Averroës (Ibn Rushd, 1126-98). The increasing availability of Aristotle's teachings shook the intellect of thirteenth-century Europe. "The Philosopher," the model of human perfection, completer of human science and author of a system that was the supreme truth, appeared through his Moorish interpreters to stand for propositions destructive of the very foundations of Christianity. Averroës had taken a statement in the third book of Aristotle's *De anima* "as meaning that there is one immortal intellect which enters into temporary union with, or performs a function in, individual men. There is therefore no personal immortality" (Copleston 1955, 171). The individual intellect survives only "a moment in the universal and common intelligence of the human species" and even while it survives it is influenced by "Intelligiencies" embodied in the various stars and in the solar system (Copleston 1950, 198).

Almost equally dangerously and, because of Aristotle's prestige, equally seductively, Averroës took "the Philosopher" to mean that matter was coeternal with God, who drew or educed from it the forms of material entities. "The order of creation or generation of material things" was "determined." Since his arguments for the eternity of matter and his denial of personal immortality were as offensive to Islam as they were to thirteenth-

6 / The Limits of Knowledge: "The Eye of Allah" 111

century Christianity, Averroës tried to evade the charge of heresy by formulating the third of his "pernicious" doctrines, that of the "double truth" of science and theology. Under this guise, one might assert a scientific or philosophical truth and simultaneously affirm one's belief in a theological proposition that appeared to contradict it, since "the picture-teaching of the Koran expresses the truth in a manner intelligible to ordinary man, to the unlettered, whereas the philosopher strips away the allegorical husk and attains the truth 'unvarnished'" (224). Although the Andalusian "caliph" Yaqub Al Mansur, acting as the instrument of orthodox Islam, condemned these doctrines as damnable and ordered all available books on logic and metaphysics to be burned, Averroës's influence on Europe was very great. After Michael Scott, court astrologer of the Emperor Frederick II, translated him in the thirteen century, Averroës was taken up, especially by the Franciscans, the order to which Roger Bacon, who appears in Kipling's story, belonged. (Bacon was writing his *Opus Majus, Opus Minus, and Opus Tertium,* with their praise of experiment, in spite of a prohibition by St. Bonaventure, at the supposed time of "The Eye of Allah.") Averroës provided ammunition for a "large body of unprofessional free-thinkers who denied immortality" (Russell 1971, 419). Hardly surprisingly, the papacy promptly recognized the danger. Translations of Averroës were forbidden by Pope Innocent III as early as 1209 (Kantorowicz 1957, 339) and Michael Scott had the same sinister reputation among orthodox Christians as Frederick II had, for many of the same reasons. (Dante consigns Scott to Hell as a magician and necromancer [*Inferno,* canto 20, lines 115–17].)

The doctrine that Stephen de Sautré remembers "the physicians at Cairo" (Kipling 1926, 394) drawing from the microscope was almost certainly some variant of Averroism. The "devils in blank" in the margin of John of Burgos's picture of the Gadarene swine are disturbing *not* because they are obviously evil, having a place in the divine scheme, even if they are explicitly banished from it, but because they are, like Averroës's eternal uncreated matter, "things as yet uninspired by Evil indifferent, but lawlessly outside imagination" (385). Kipling underlines the point by contrasting the painting of the Gadarene swine with John's other picture, that of the Magdalen. In the latter, painted without the aid of the microscope, the seven devils are the colors of evil as the medieval mind was accustomed to them, from phosphorescent green to the "black purple of outworn iniquity" (384). The iniquity is "outworn" because of the triumph of Christ and the Church, symbolized in the conventionalized spring flowers of the deep border "drawn for the sign of hope and the sane workings of life" (384).

It was the idea of the eternity of matter that the medieval intellect found intolerable. It is this which Stephen de Sautré recalls when he again sees the "shapes" in the drop of water under the microscope: "They are here—as they were in my time—my time past. There is no end to them. I was told. . . . There *is* no end" (388–89). Such apparent evidence of an eternal universe confirms another of the dangerous Averroist tenets: the rejection of personal immortality. The abbot recalls this also from his time in Cairo. "It was shown to me in Cairo," says the abbot to himself, "that man stands ever between two infinities—of greatness and littleness. Therefore, there is no end—either to life—or" (390). The word he is about to add, "death," and the connotations it carries in this context are implied by Roger of Salerno's bitter rejoinder, "And *I* stand on the verge of the grave. . . . Who pities me?" (390)

Given the horror the "Averroist" teachings had aroused, it may well seem that they provide a sufficient reason for the breaking of the microscope. Stephen de Sautré has undoubtedly perceived one essential point about his own society, perhaps about any society, that when it encounters that which is "outside the rational mind" (385)—outside, that is, its own perception of reality—it reacts by labeling the unknown as "evil." The Church would "frame" the unbearable knowledge as "hell of devils contending in the compass of one drop of water" (393). Intellectual schemes, religions, or cultures survive as orders, fronting the banked shoals of sunset or the sea of dreams, by locking their gates, as the abbey is symbolically made "fast" (377) for the night ("Make it so till Prime"). They must exclude by their very nature.

There are two other features in the situation that give it an added resonance. The simpler of these is the fact that minute organisms revealed by the microscope offer light "concerning the causes of things," including, as Roger of Salerno tells the abbot, "thy Lady's—thine own Lady's—eating malady" (392). Stephen's reply that he has indeed thought of this gives him a tragic stature. The point is that what is at stake is too great to be sacrificed even in return for medical discoveries that would spare others the bereavement he is about to undergo.

The second nuance is added by a knowledge of Kipling's own strong sympathy with modern variants of "Averroism," specifically with the belief that "influences" pervade the universe and have something to do with its structure, we being part of it. For example, he remarked approvingly in an after-dinner speech to the Royal Society of Medicine in November 1928 that Nicholas Culpeper, hero of his own story "A Doctor of Medicine,"

6 / The Limits of Knowledge: "The Eye of Allah"

would find the "essential unity of creation" supported by modern scientific research, "and that man, Culpeper's epitome of all, is himself a universe of universes, each ordered—negatively and positively—by sympathy and antipathy—on the same lines as hold the stars in their courses" (quoted in Dobrée 1969, 26). The poem "The Threshold" that concludes "Unprofessional" (a story that deals with healing by such influences) in *Limits and Renewals* offers an explicitly "Averroist" model of the universe, emphasizing the educing of being from eternal, not created, matter. "The Threshold" celebrates the "crystal eyed Sages of Ionia," the pre-Socratics, for having

> proved one Matter in all things—
> Eternal, changeless, unseen
> "That the heart of the Matter was single
> Till the Breath should bring it forth.["]
>
> (Kipling 1932, 284)

Kipling regarded what was rejected in "The Eye of Allah" as philosophical and religious wisdom and "truth" as well as a useful scientific and medical discovery. This being so, it adds to the pathos and magnanimity of the story that it should suggest the rejection is not merely expedient and necessary, but right. What Kipling saw as permanent truth, or as near to it as man could reach (since "there is an unscientific objection on the part of the First Cause to being inquired of" [Kipling 1923]), cannot be allowed to appear prematurely to damage a civilization that was at its ripest and most creative.

However, there are further recesses in Stephen de Sautré's character and experience, and a further twist to his motives, beyond an unhappy love affair and likely general fear of Averroism. By setting the love story when he does, Kipling has, in fact, chosen a date when the fear of Averroism was *diminishing*. The recent controversial triumph of Thomas Aquinas over its latest proponent, Siger of Brabant, had greatly weakened the attraction of European intellectuals towards the skeptical teachings derived from the Moslem commentators on Aristotle. The theological context of "The Eye of Allah" was not pessimistic and fearful but one that "justified a full confidence in man" and in his natural tendency perfected by God's grace to "knowledge and full love of the Divine" (Gardner 1979, 75). It is possible that this is the theological climate that lies behind the liberal atmosphere of St. Illod's monastery.

The fact that Stephen permits John of Burgos's journey to Spain, from which the Averroist commentaries had originated, implies that he is not afraid of Moorish culture as such, at least in its Andalusian form, or even of what would now be called cultural "cross-fertilization." Indeed, at the date of "The Eye of Allah," Alphonso the Wise of Castile (1252–84) was carrying out a programme of translation in which a vast number of works from Arabic were made available by Jewish assistants. John is made to justify the king's tolerance on grounds of expediency. If they chased the Moors and Jews away "they'd be no trade nor farming" (370). More significantly, he is made to delight in one of the architectural triumphs of this cultural amalgamation. His comment that the new cathedral at Burgos is "good for the soul" (366) is interesting in this context, since the glory of the building, the triforium, is an outstanding blend of French and Moorish work. It is hardly surprising, given such aesthetic inclusiveness, that John should feel no embarrassment in using "wholesome" Moorish diaper work (366) to draw the eye toward his picture of a Christian mystery, the Annunciation.

Stephen de Sautré sees no danger in such artistic borrowings from the infidels and makes no attempt to prevent them, in the easy climate of the conquered lands Granada way. His own experience in Cairo, however, was of a different order. After many years, the sight of the microscope, in "The Eye of Allah," triggers a fear that is indeed more than a general suspicion of the now defeated Averroism or the troubling ghost of a love across the barriers of race and religion, although, with a characteristic late-Kipling sense of the density of character and motive, we are allowed to see that these other elements do color Stephen's mind. The clue to what the "trigger" is lies in a casual reference, dropped early in the story, to an "unlucky crusade" and "a battle at Mansura" (367). The understatement is eloquent, since the name is enough to carry an inevitable train of associations.

The battle at Mansura (8 February 1250) was fought during the expedition of Louis IX against Egypt and forms an incident in one of the best known and most readable of all medieval biographies, Joinville's *Life of Saint Louis*. Kipling's own knowledge of the French classics, of which this is one, was, of course, outstanding and it seems likely that he would have agreed with his "literary patron" George Saintsbury, "the old critic he treated with deep respect" and with whom his discussions "turned mostly on French literature" (Carrington 1970, 552), that "all persons who have even a slight knowledge of French literature must be aware how early and how remarkable are its possessions in what is vaguely called the 'Memoir' department" (Saintsbury 1917, 1:135). Saintsbury goes on to assert that there

6 / The Limits of Knowledge: "The Eye of Allah"

was nothing similar "at the time, in any modern literature" to Joinville's achievement, and to praise the early historian's power of rendering "pure personal experience" and his "indefinable gift" of "telling a story." They are the qualities Kipling would have found particularly valuable.

Interestingly, the critical book in which Saintsbury's remarks appeared (part 1 of *A History of the French Novel*) was read by Kipling on a "superior sort of Whitsuntide holiday" (Carrington 1970, 552), in which he did nothing at all except read and compare notes about French literature with his cousin Stanley Baldwin ("I haven't had as good a time for years"). This was three years before he wrote "The Eye of Allah." The casual way in which he drops in the reference suggests that he expected at least some of his readers to catch it. Indeed, Joinville is hardly esoteric. A translation had appeared in 1908 in the popular Everyman Library edition, with a stirring introduction by Sir Theodore Marzials, and was often reprinted.

Joinville's account of St. Louis's Crusade is interesting for several reasons that are relevant to Stephen de Sautré and "The Eye of Allah." Perhaps the keynote of the whole of this famous and vivid record of the disaster at Mansura is the contrast it draws between the simple piety of the Crusaders and the technological superiority of their opponents. Louis IX undertook the Crusade out of gratitude for his miraculous recovery from illness. On learning of his decision his queen, understandably, "mourned as much as if she had seen him lying dead" (Joinville and Villehardouin 1969, 191).

Joinville was not a self-conscious artist. His personal reminiscences were dictated, not written, and bear the marks of an old man's repetitions. What makes his testimony especially interesting is its combination of sharp detail and a conventional, devout mind. The only explanation he offers for the French disaster is that the Crusaders "Forgot God their Saviour" (206). However, the many facts he himself notices provide more immediate reasons. The sultan's army enjoyed an enormous numerical superiority; "The din this army made with its kettledrums and horns was terrifying to hear" (201). More to the purpose, the Moslem soldiers had skills for which the French had no answer, notably an ability to infiltrate their enemies' camp: "The Saracens came every night into our camp on foot and killed our men where they found them sleeping" (209). Mounted patrols were ineffective, since the Moslems would "creep into the camp behind the horses." In this context, it is interesting that Kipling should single out Stephen de Sautré's power of silent movement as his first notable characteristic and should state that he learned this technique among the Moslems.

The sultan's army soon demonstrates a terrifying range of inventions and armaments that completely outclass the Crusaders. They bring forward, for example, "a machine called a petrary, which they had not done before, and put Greek fire into its sling" (215). This Greek fire (the medieval equivalent of napalm) devastates the French army.

Joinville frequently mentions these and other infidel "machines" (215 or 237, for example) and touches on the superiority of Moslem engineering to that of his own side ("In one day they undid all we had done in three week's labour" [214]). He suggests, too, that the infidel commanders had better-disciplined troops and a more scientific strategy than those of his own side. (They tackled one French detachment, he remarks with awe, "in the way that men play chess" [231].) Although he asserts on one occasion, with touching loyalty, that the prayers of "our saintly king" did "us good service in our need" (216), these religious aids are ultimately inadequate protection against a highly mechanized, superbly equipped opponent. The French knights are outmaneuvered, pinned down, and overwhelmed by a Moslem army that their ideal of individual prowess has given them no psychological preparation to encounter. (Joinville celebrates one battle as a "noble passage of arms" [222] because it involves no bows or crossbows, much less the dreaded "machines.")

The devices employed by the Saracens to win their victory in 1250 provide a scientific context for that other strange discovery, "The Eye of Allah," which Stephen de Sautré is supposed to see in Cairo during his imprisonment. However, it is the strange events, recorded by Joinville, that follow the French defeat that suggest a more subtle set of connotations. After he and his king were made prisoner, Joinville entered a world whose essential quality was one of fragmentation. This section of the *Life of Saint Louis* gives the reader the impression that there is nothing the Saracens will not do and no way of knowing what they will do next. There appears to be no stable perception or moral center to their lives. Instead, there are fleeting displays of attitudes and actions that may be striking in themselves but that are utterly inconsistent with each other.

One Moslem, at some danger to himself, saves Joinville's life. When he becomes ill, imagining that he has "a tumour of the throat," one of the Saracen knights gives him "something to drink" (244) that cures him in two days. Another "old Saracen Knight" cares for his sick friend Raoul de Wanou, carrying him "pick-a-back to the privy whenever he so required" (245). In addition to these courtesies, the Moslems show a solicitude for their captives' spiritual comfort. The Saracens' admiral gently assures

6 / The Limits of Knowledge: "The Eye of Allah"

Joinville that God will not hold his eating meat on Friday against him, as he did so in ignorance (245). Seeing that their French prisoners are growing despondent, "a great crowd of young Saracens" (247) (whom Joinville wrongly assumes are going to cut off their heads) rush into their pavilion, bringing with them an aged and white-haired holy man. He assures them that if they suffer for Christ, "dying" for his sake as he died for them, he has the power to deliver them.

Yet, at the same time, the infidels methodically slaughter those of their prisoners who have become helpless through sickness. The admiral who had consoled Joinville for eating meat on Friday explains "that the men in question did not count, because the sickness which they suffered left them incapable of doing anything to help themselves" (245–46). Such an attitude serves as an example of what the Averroist doctrine of "double truth" might well amount to in action. It is clearly different from what Kipling himself meant when he celebrated having two separate sides to his head in "The Two-Sided Man." The "double truth" Joinville's captors exhibited was not an acceptance of different points of view or different angles of vision. Rather, it was an ability to entertain (and to enjoy the satisfactions of) entirely contradictory sets of values. A concern for spirituality and a readiness to slit throats on "scientific" principles coexist in the same world, often in the same people.

As is well known, St. Louis's imprisonment by the Saracens coincided with a coup d'état and the murder of the sultan by his own emirs. Joinville's account records his own and his companions' horror at one of the worst crimes the feudal mind could envisage, the murder of one's lord. However, the assassination takes place in a society where treachery, as the only means of self-preservation, has become the normal and almost accepted rule. The sultan's "special reward" for the "distinguished service" of victorious subordinate commanders, in Joinville's ironic phrase, is to have them "put to death, and their wives deprived of everything they possess" (236). On this occasion the emirs anticipate him, pointing out, as they hack him to pieces, that "as you say we wish to kill you, it's better to do it than let ourselves be killed by you" (251). Joinville's account of what follows the battle of Mansura depicts a way of life from which all coherence has gone. The thoughts and feelings of the sophisticated, technologically advanced Egyptian society of the thirteenth century exist in fragments. Wholeness is nowhere to be found. The emirs, erratic to the point of phantasmagoria, plan to kill Louis IX, or alternatively to make him, though a Christian, sultan of Egypt. Swearing oaths and breaking them with equal facility (to Joinville's bewilderment [256]), they decide the fate of their captives with a curious blend of political expediency and texts from the Koran. One final and weird detail captures their utter inconstancy. Having decided, almost by a whim, to release their prisoners, the emirs, feeling "shamed" that their prisoners should depart fasting, will not let them go until they have eaten a simple meal of cheese fritters and hard-boiled eggs, "the shells of which, in our honour, had been painted in various colours" (257).

Joinville's record, all the more telling because it is unanalytical and "naive," gives substance and specificity to Stephen de Sautré's memory of his time among the infidels in "The Eye of Allah." It would, above all, be a memory of disconnection, of religious visionaries and "scientific" murderers, held together by no shared belief or code. The white-haired old man who consoles the Christians with a moving account of their own beliefs and the old woman who roams the streets proclaiming that man should love God for Himself alone (274) exist in the same place with, and throw no light upon, the Saracen knight who tears out the sultan's heart and comes to Louis IX "with his hand all dripping with blood," demanding a reward (252).

The abbot's destruction of the microscope in Kipling's tale is set in a context of shifting lights and delicately unspecified motives. Both "The Eye of Allah" and Joinville's history, with its record of the Christian apostate who married an Egyptian and lived "rich and at ease" (262) but knowing he was damned, suggest the sorrow of love across the barrier of different faiths. Yet, while this may set up the emotional basis for Stephen's breaking of "the Eye of Allah," it is not what triggers his action.

"The Eye of Allah" gives that reason, with a skillful allusiveness, just before the denouement of the story. Kipling has already embodied the balance of forces within the medieval Christian vision, in John's painting of the Annunciation, and symbolized the precariousness of its order, in the image of the abbey buildings, set against the sunset. He now demonstrates it in action. Roger of Salerno, having judged it best to tell the abbot's lady she had an inoperable cancer (378), tricks out his callousness with a Latin quotation. John of Burgos mocks his pedantry. The conversation at the "Wisdom Dinner" gives him an opportunity for an even more effective rejoinder. Roger holds forth on the failure to test authority by experiment and instances Apuleius's assertion that "if a man eat fasting of the juice of the cut-leaved buttercup" he will die laughing, when, of course, he will die with his own mouth convulsed by a rictus. John simply remarks, from his own artist's experience, that this statement was probably a lazy copyist's

6 / The Limits of Knowledge: "The Eye of Allah"

"short-cut" (382), in leaving out a "seems to" from Apuleius's statement. In any case, he adds, deflating Roger still further, every child knows how to use the cut-leaved buttercup. He himself used it in feigning illness "to save going to prayer o'cold nights" (382).

Stephen de Sautré's 'Wisdom Dinner' demonstrates the checking of one specialism by another, the value of a unified culture compared to a world of "double truth." Roger Bacon can view the splitting of light "on the rim of a crystal salt-cellar" (379), Roger of Salerno can discuss spotted fever, and John of Burgos "can take note of the keen profile" for a drawing of St. Luke the physician. Yet, unlike the Saracens of Joinville's fragmented world, they can do so (at least, in 1267) within the confines of one moral and intellectual frame of reference. When, by Stephen de Sautré's order, each man looks into the microscope and offers his own response, the effect is almost one of a ritual of disintegration. Roger of Salerno rails bitterly against God and the Church as the enemies of new life and thought. Roger Bacon, turning "the apparatus in his capable hands" (389), is obviously considering its purely technical aspects. Thomas the infirmarian flings himself, with a mystic's delight, into "life created and rejoicing" and begins hysterically to chant the "Benedicite Omnia Opera." John of Burgos cares only for the new shapes he can exploit in his art.

Perhaps Stephen intended his ritual to prove the point to himself. In any case, the abbot, his eyes "on times past," can see demonstrated before him the beginnings of the nightmare in which, as the reference to Joinville suggests, he must have lived after Mansura. He has his reasons, based on those memories, for believing that the invention at that time would be "the mother of more death, more torture, more division in this dark age" (394). In suggesting what his motives were for destroying the "Eye of Allah," Kipling demonstrates not merely the psychological perception and deliberate ambivalence all readers detect and most readers admire in his later fiction, but a depth of historical and cultural understanding less often noticed but equally striking.

7
Kipling's Valediction to Art: "Proofs of Holy Writ"

"Proofs of Holy Writ" (1934), Kipling's last important story, which never appeared in any of his collections, has been much praised and enjoyed. It is arguable that the praise was wide of the mark and the enjoyment unconnected with serious literary qualities. The story reflects the scholarly interests of Kipling's late period, those increasingly learned tastes that were partly the outgrowth and partly the cause of his friendship with George Saintsbury (Carrington 1970, 551–52). It would certainly be foolish to suggest that antiquarian interests in late Kipling were necessarily a sign of a loss of creative power. Such interests vary in their intrinsic quality and in the use to which he put them. There is, for example, a world of difference between the parodies of Horace and the use of medieval material in "Dayspring Mishandled" (in *Limits and Renewals*).

Nevertheless, a picture of Shakespeare and Ben Jonson in the "relaxed atmosphere of peace in the shady garden of old age" (as Roger Lancelyn Green puts it [1970, xix]), in which the two old friends discuss the rendering of a passage from the Vulgate, might well seem to lack artistic concentration and fictional interest.

"Proofs of Holy Writ" might plausibly be viewed as a diversion by and for an elderly bookman. It is in these terms that it is dismissed by Angus Wilson: "It is the sort of piece of old-fashioned dons' recreation which is usually called 'delightful,' and so it is, but no more" (1977, 331). Besides, the piece could be said to lack originality. The conversation of Jonson and Shakespeare seems to draw on the by now traditional picture, originally given by Fuller in *The Worthies of England* (1662). Clearly Kipling has derived an important element of the exchange between the two playwrights from Fuller's description of how they joined battle,

7 / Kipling's Valediction to Art: "Proofs of Holy Writ"

like a Spanish great galleon and an English man-of-war; Master Jonson . . . was built far higher in learning, but slow in his performances. Shakespeare . . . lesser in bulk but light in sailing could turn with all tides, tack about and take advantage of all winds. (Quoted in Quennell 1969, 298)

This is obviously an important element in the picture Kipling presents. The point is that it is only one element.

Once this preliminary point about the groundwork of Kipling's characterization in "Proofs of Holy Writ" has been made, it is possible to see how much more subtle and serious short fiction it is than its use of a traditional model would be first suggest. Nominally a comparison of different translations, concerned with certain finer points in the rendering of Latin into English, it is, essentially, a study of the nature of art and of the artist. Handling a subject that, above many others, might easily lend itself to windy affirmations and turgid generalities, it does not put a foot wrong. "Proof of Holy Writ" manages to be serious and at the same time delicate and tactful.

The conversation opens with the briefest of introductions, which nevertheless indicates more than a mere difference in physique between the two men. Jonson's "broad face blotched and scarred" and the way he "puffed a little as he came to rest" (Kipling 1970, 178) are contrasted with Shakespeare's easy picking of an apple from the grass and relaxed taking up of the thread of talk. An important nuance in the dialogue is the presence or absence of peace of mind. One man, we are to feel, has it. The other has not. Drawing on *Conversations with Drummond of Hawthornden,* Kipling sketches Jonson's feuds with rival poets such as Dekker and Marston. Why, Shakespeare asks, does he "waste time fighting atomies who do not come up to your belly-button?" (178). Jonson insists that he finds it stimulating: "You'd be better for a tussle or two" (178).

Here occurs Kipling's first significant alteration of his sources. In *Timber or Discoveries,* Jonson's criticism of Shakespeare's plays had been one of lack of economy, "wherein he flowed with that facility, that sometime it was necessary he should be stopped" (Jonson 1951, 36).

In "Proofs of Holy Writ," this is deliberately reversed. However, one might note the much less familiar view of a contemporary, Leonard Digges, that Jonson's *Sejanus* was "laboured" (quoted in Halliday 1963, 54) and tedious, as Shakespeare describes it in "Proofs of Holy Writ." Shakespeare remarks of Jonson's *Bartholomew Fair:* "It creaks like an overloaded haywain. . . . You give too much" (Kipling 1970, 178).

This reversal is an important clue to the meaning of the story. Kipling makes Shakespeare, both here and elsewhere in the tale, tend to that stringent economy which, after about 1900, was his own firmest conviction about the art of writing:

> In an auspicious hour, read your final draft and consider faithfully every paragraph, sentence and word, blacking out where requisite. Let it lie by to drain as long as possible. At the end of that time, re-read and you should find that it will bear a second shortening. (Kipling 1990, 121)

The implication of the alteration of the source seems inescapable. Kipling is offering not only this but several other of his views of art through the mouth of Shakespeare. Shakespeare takes issue with Jonson not only as a diffuse author but as a highbrow with a self-conscious mission to improve the intellectual level of the public:

> They should be taught, then—taught."
> "Always that? What's your commission to enlighten us?" (178)

Jonson is the exponent of the teaching role of art, of an art demanding in its attitude to its audience, priding itself on the originality of its conceptions and on its laborious and thorough construction. Art ought, it appears, to show its pains. It should be strenuous, cerebral, and architectonic:

> "I deny nothing of my brain-store to my lines. I–I build up my own works throughout." (179)

(Through the piece, the hint of shortness of breath or puffing in Jonson's speech rhythm recalls that initial, and possibly spiritual, lack of ease.) Jonson insists that he is continually breaking new ground. Shakespeare rejects the continual demand to be original as a necessary adjunct to the artist's task. Jonson urges, and Shakespeare denies, the need for a careful scholarly accuracy in attempts to re-create past times, events, or characters, as in "my Sejanus, of which the mob was unworthy" (179).

It is this last challenge to Shakespeare's approach and temper on which the story turns, since its subject essentially is the problem of cultural continuity through translation. The contrast between the two is not meant to be a simple one of highbrow and lowbrow writers or between a self-consciously intellectual art and an instinctive craft of the theater. At the start of the story, in a glancing way that might easily be missed, Shakespeare remarks

7 / Kipling's Valediction to Art: "Proofs of Holy Writ" 123

that one of his four reasons for avoiding a quarrel with Jonson is simply "betterment of this present age" (178). It is a hint that he has in fact deeper ends in view, although, unlike Jonson, he does not choose to be articulate and programmatic about them. The opening of the dialogue is a gentle yet effective critique of a magisterial view of the nature and function of art.

The first point Shakespeare, and through him Kipling, makes is that the artist as teacher, corrector of morals and manners, and maintainer and promoter of cultural standards enjoys no peace, since his ostensible aims prevent his examining his own touchiness and amour propre, which are his principal, though hidden, motives. As a stance, the magisterial "intellectual" position is ineffective since it solicits ridicule. When Jonson offers, as his "commission" to instruct,

> "My own learning which I have heaped up, lifelong ... My assured knowledge, also, of my craft and art,"

the reply is definitive:

> "The one sure road to mockery." (179)

Shakespeare is rarely quite as sharp as this. In fact, it is part of Kipling's approach to make him pull his punches. Throughout the exchange with Jonson he reminds him, from time to time, that the bottle is at his elbow. There is a suggestion of a pervasive kindliness, but also of tact in plying his guest with drink. Jonson recognizes the "bribery." Notwithstanding, it is effective. The edge of a potential quarrel is blunted.

Yet the point about Jonson's self-deception loses nothing in acuteness. He complains bitterly that Dekker has referred to him as a "hodman" because his stepfather was a bricklayer. Shakespeare reminds him that he shows the mentality of a builder, brick by brick, in his plays. When later, Jonson scornfully remarks that the divine, Miles Smith, was the son of a butcher, the response is a polite "Is it so?" (181), an obvious, if understated, reaction.

Skillfully and in a brief space, Kipling sketches Shakespeare's relationships with Miles Smith, with Dick Burbage (who has taken the leading role in his plays), with the servant who has brought Smith's request for help, and with Jonson. The common factors in all of them are a human interest and a quiet indulgence. Something is implied in his motioning the drunken servant to stretch himself on the grass; more in his remark that

"Yon's a business I've neglected all this day for thy fat sake—and he by so much the drunker" (180).

It seems that he has been treating him as he has been treating Jonson, calming the boredom of one and the exacerbated vanity of the other, by the same means. He wishes, too, to spare the tipsy messenger an interrogation from his friend, in whom "a nosing Justice of the Peace" (180) was lost. After these little hints of an easy, accommodating temper, it seems natural to learn that the characterization and the themes of some of his major plays were responses to the personal and acting needs of Burbage:

> "my *Hamlet* that I botched for him when he had staled of our Kings. . . . And when poor Dick was at odds with the world in general and womenkind in special, I clapped him up my *Lear* for a vomit. . . . And when he'd come out of his whoremongering aftermaths of repentance I served him my *Macbeth* to toughen him. . . ." (180)

Shakespeare's tolerance, his refusal to judge, are most marked in the case of "the most learned divine, Miles Smith of Brazen Nose College." Jonson is quick to detect a slight, which Shakespeare characteristically passes over, in this personage's having "withheld his name" on the outside of his letter. Smith is something of a test. A pompous academic, in whom Jonson can see only vanity and pretension, he has been touched by Macbeth's lines beginning, "Tomorrow and tomorrow and tomorrow." As Shakespeare recalls, "He said they were, to his godly apprehension, a parable, as it might be, of his reverend self, going down darkling to his tomb 'twixt cliffs of ice and iron" (181).

The function of art is to touch the egotism, or speak to the hidden fears, of such a complacent minor functionary as Smith. Where Jonson's scolding and correcting would have merely antagonized the Oxford divine, Shakespeare's conception of art allows of the possibility of contact. It also gives the reason for his advice being sought over the translation of a passage of Isaiah.

Clearly then, the act of translation, upon which "Proofs of Holy Writ" turns, takes place in an emotional context. Shakespeare's understanding of the text has been carefully prepared for, connected as it is with his sympathy with all kinds of men. Two points are most noticeable about his method. They are his reliance on what he calls his "Demon," and his sympathetic, imaginatively interpretative manner of approaching Isaiah. The "Demon," of course, forcibly recalls Kipling himself:

7 / Kipling's Valediction to Art: "Proofs of Holy Writ"

My Daemon was with me in the *Jungle Books, Kim* and both Puck books, and good care I took to walk delicately, lest he should withdraw. . . . When your Daemon is in charge, do not try to think consciously. Drift, wait and obey. (1990, 122–23)

Shakespeare's reverence for his "Demon" ("Quiet, man!" said he. "I wait on my Demon!") is combined with a somewhat ruthless use of Jonson's learning. This he battens on, in the course of his translation, avoiding any slips of verbal accuracy in the rendering, while transmuting and revitalizing the whole by a grasping at the inward spirit of what Isaiah is saying. He conceives the prophet as in a dramatic role:

"[W]hat's the colour and use of this cursed *caligo,* Ben? '*Et caligo populos.*'"
"'Mistiness' or, as in Pliny, 'blindness.' And further—"
"No-o. . . . 'Shadow' and 'mist' are not men enough for this work. . . . Blindness did ye say, Ben? . . . The blackness atop of mere darkness?" (183)

The whole effort amounts to a welding together of scholarly information into a newly created whole through an instinctive grasp of the personality behind the words and of the occasion of their utterance:

"But Isaiah's prophesying, with the storm behind him. Can ye not *feel* it, Ben? It must be 'shall.'" (183)

Shakespeare, when called upon to interpret the past, makes use of the nearest approximation in the present. Thus, when he had had to translate Ezekiel "making mock of fallen Tyrus in his twenty-seventh chapter,"

"I took it to the Bank—four o'clock of a summer morn; stretched out in one of our wherries—and watched London, Port and Town, up and down the river, waking all arrayed to heap more upon evident excess." (187)

Coupled with this reliance on intuition is an exacting care for sound and cadence. Throughout his joint exercise with Jonson, he is continually repeating and assessing verbal rhythms, the alignment and fall of the spoken word. He cares little or nothing for the terms of rhetoric used to describe these effects, for the apparatus of criticism. To Jonson's reproach that he does not know "the names of the tools of his trade," of "the measures and pulses of strong words," Shakespeare replies that it is his business to create, his friend's to label: "I beget some such stuff and send it to you to christen" (185).

One intriguing point about the portrait of the ideal artist (for that is what it surely is) that Kipling offers is the contrast between Shakespeare's lack of egotism, his relaxed, undemanding attitudes to friends or casual contacts, and the way in which he stiffens into a rigorous hardness in the service of his "Demon." This, it is clear, brings him on to a higher level of consciousness. When he has translated the passage he falls back into a benign quietude, encouraging Jonson to talk about his theories and grievances.

Yet the two qualities of the artist, the human sympathy and the "Demon," are shown as clearly related. Lying behind them both, and perhaps feeding both kinds of sympathy, are a sense of the losses time has brought ("I've gained and lost enough—lost enough" [187]), a curious lack of interest in whether the work he has produced will endure, and a sorrowful envy of Marlowe, the lost friend killed "when all the world was young" and his only possible rival. (These dispositions may, perhaps, be a slight allusion to some of Kipling's concerns: the loss of two children and the early death of his great friend Wolcott Balestier.)

"Proofs of Holy Writ" is important for what it suggests of Kipling's view of the art of writing, in his valediction to it. In a significant way, it supplements the notion of the "daemon" that in the canonical account, in *Something of Myself,* is somewhat unsatisfactory. There the impression is one of a willful irrationalism, of letting oneself be taken over, almost of a kind of automatic writing, in which the individual personality is nothing, the "daemon" everything. "Proofs of Holy Writ" corrects this. The "Shakespearian" quality of day-to-day personal response, by freeing the artist from vanity and self-concern, allows him to receive the "daemon." In another sense it *is* the "daemon," since the sympathy, diffused in mundane acts of tact, in a concentrated form is the energy of artistic creation.

Both aspects of the "Shakespearian" mind, the mind of the ideal artist Kipling aspired to be, are alien to the Jonsonian temper, the judging, categorizing, theorizing intellect. It has been pointed out that Kipling, until his last years, remained ill at ease with intellectuals (Wilson 1977, 330–31), with the academic and literary world that included many of his bitterest critics. In "Proofs of Holy Writ," the animosity he felt toward them has modulated into a gentler and more cogently expressed attitude. The figure

7 / Kipling's Valediction to Art: "Proofs of Holy Writ"

of Jonson is not a lampoon on the critical intellectual temper, but an attempt to put it literally in its place, a place assistant to but definitely inferior to artistic creation.

The resulting piece of short fiction has a control of tone not perhaps usually associated with Kipling. Its creation of character, atmosphere, and period, its convincing, unpretentious sketch of creation in act and its deeper seriousness, blend with its surface pleasures, the portrait of two old friends nodding in a shady garden, the mellow civilized tone. After so many stories involving reconciliation in his last period, it is fitting that Kipling should have reconciled art and intellectualism, himself and his critics.

Bibliography

Amis, K. 1975. *Rudyard Kipling and His World.* London: Thames and Hudson.

Attridge, D., G. Bennington, and R. Young. 1988. *Poststructuralism and the Question of History.* Cambridge: Cambridge University Press.

Ballhatchet, K. 1982. *Race, Sex, and Class under the Raj.* London: Weidenfeld and Nicholson.

Belloc, H. 1912. *This and That and The Other.* London: Methuen.

Bergonzi, B. 1980. *Heroes' Twilight.* London: Macmillan.

Birkenhead, Lord. 1978. *Rudyard Kipling.* New York: Random House.

Bivona, D. 1990. *Desire and Contradiction: Imperial Divisions and Domestic Debate in Victorian Literature.* Manchester: Manchester University Press.

Bodelsen, C. H. 1964. *Aspects of Kipling's Art.* Manchester: Manchester University Press.

Brantlinger, P. 1988. *Rule of Darkness: British Literature and Imperialism.* London: Cornell University Press.

Brown, H. 1945. *Rudyard Kipling: A New Appreciation.* London: Hamish Hamilton.

Brown, Lewis, ed. 1962. *The Wisdom of Israel.* 1948. London: New English Library.

Carrington, Charles. 1970. *Rudyard Kipling: His Life and His Work.* 1955. Reprint, Harmondsworth: Penguin.

Chesterton, G. K. 1905. *Heretics.* London: The Bodley Head.

———. 1947. *The Victorian Age in Literature.* 1913. Reprint, London: Oxford University Press.

———. 1950. *The Common Man.* London: Sheed and Ward.

———. 1956. *Saint Thomas Aquinas.* 1933. Reprint, New York: Doubleday.

———. 1959. *Autobiography.* 1936. Reprint, London: Arrow Books.

Bibliography

Colls, M., and P. Dodds. 1986. *Englishness: Politics and Culture, 1880–1920.* London: Croom Helm.

Conrad, J. 1967. *Nostromo.* 1904. Reprint, Harmondsworth: Penguin.

———. 1989. *Lord Jim.* 1900. Reprint, Oxford: Oxford University Press.

Cooper, Duff. 1932. *Talleyrand.* London: Jonathan Cape.

Copleston, F. C. 1950. *A History of Philosophy.* Vol. 2. London: Burns, Oates, and Washbourne.

———. 1955. *Aquinas.* Harmondsworth: Penguin.

Cornell, L. 1966. *Kipling in India.* London: Macmillan.

Crook, Nora. 1989. *Kipling's Myths of Love and Death.* London: Macmillan.

Crossley-Holland, Kevin. 1982. *The Norse Myths.* 1980. Reprint, Harmondsworth: Penguin.

Davidson, Hilda Ellis. 1964. *Gods and Myths of Northern Europe.* Harmondsworth: Penguin.

Dobrée, Bonamy. 1969. *Rudyard Kipling, Realist and Fabulist.* London and New York: Oxford University Press, 1969.

Doyle, Sir Arthur Conan. 1951. *The Conan Doyle Stories.* 1929. Reprint, London: John Murray.

Eby, C. 1988. *The Road to Armageddon: The Martial Spirit in English Literature, 1830–1914.* Durham, N.C.: Duke University Press.

Eldridge, C. 1973. *England's Mission: The Imperial Idea in the Age of Gladstone and Disraeli, 1868–1880.* London: Macmillan.

Eliade, Mircea. 1972. *Myths, Dreams, and Mysteries.* 1957. Reprint, London: Fontana.

Eliot, T. S., ed. 1973. *A Choice of Kipling's Verse.* 1941. Reprint, London: Faber & Faber.

Ellis, John M. 1989. *Against Deconstruction.* Princeton: Princeton University Press.

Faber, R., 1966. *The Vision and the Need: Late Victorian Imperialist Aims.* London: Faber & Faber.

Fido, M. 1974. *Rudyard Kipling.* London: Hamlyn.

Field, H. J. 1982. *Toward a Programme of Imperial Life: The British Empire at the Turn of the Century.* Chicago: Greenwood Press.

Gardner, John. 1979. *The Life and Times of Chaucer.* 1977. Reprint, St. Albans: Granada Publishing.

Gilbert, E. 1972. *The Good Kipling: Studies in the Short Story.* Manchester: Manchester University Press.

Grant, Michael. 1976. *Saint Paul.* London: Weidenfeld and Nicholson.

Green, M. 1980. *Dreams of Adventure: Deeds of Empire.* New York: Basic Books.

Green, Roger Lancelyn. 1965. *Kipling and the Children.* London: Elek.

———. 1970. Introduction to *Rudyard Kipling: Stories and Poems.* Edited by Roger Lancelyn Green. London: Dent.

———. 1971. *Kipling: The Critical Heritage.* London: Routledge and Kegan Paul.

Grass, J., ed. 1975. *Rudyard Kipling: The Man, His Work, and His World.* London: Weidenfeld and Nicholson.

Halliday, F. E. 1963. *Shakespeare and His Critics.* 1958. Reprint, New York: Schocken Books.

Heer, F. 1963. *The Medieval World.* Translated by Janet Sondheimer. 1962. Reprint, New York: New American Library.

Henn, T. R. 1967. *Kipling.* Edinburgh: Oliver and Boyd.

Hutchins, F. 1967. *The Illusion of Permanence: British Imperialism in India.* Princeton: Princeton University Press.

Islam, Shamsul. 1975. *Kipling's Law: A Study of His Philosophy of Life.* London: Macmillan.

James, Henry. 1962. "The Art of Fiction." 1884. Reprinted in *The House of Fiction,* edited by Leon Edel. London: Heinemann.

James Rhodes, R. 1978. *The British Revolution: British Politics, 1880–1930.* London: Methuen.

Joinville, Jean de, and Geoffroy de Villehardouin. 1969. *Chronicles of the Crusades.* Translated by M. R. B. Shaw. Harmondsworth: Penguin.

Jonson, Ben. 1951. *Timber, or Discoveries made upon Men and Matters.* London: Dent.

Kantorowicz, Ernst. 1957. *Frederick the Second, 1194–1250.* Translated by E. O. Lorimer. 1931. Reprint, London: Constable and Co.

Kemp, Sandra. 1989. *Kipling's Hidden Narratives.* Oxford: Basil Blackwell.

Kipling, Rudyard. 1889. "In Partibus." Quoted in Charles Carrington, *Rudyard Kipling: His Life and His Work* (1955; reprint, Harmondsworth: Penguin, 1970), 187.

———. 1892. *Life's Handicap.* 1891. Reprint, London: Macmillan.

———. 1907. *Plain Tales from the Hills.* 1890. Reprint, London: Macmillan.

———. 1909. *Actions and Reactions.* London: Macmillan.

———. 1910. *Rewards and Fairies.* London: Macmillan.

———. 1923. "Rectorial Address at St Andrews." Quoted by Bonamy Dobrée, *Rudyard Kipling, Realist and Fabulist* (London and New York: Oxford University Press, 1969), 24.

———. 1926. *Debits and Credits.* London: Macmillan.

———. 1928. *A Book of Words.* London: Macmillan.

———. 1930. *Puck of Pook's Hill.* 1906. Reprint, London: Macmillan.

———. 1932. *Limits and Renewals.* London: Macmillan.

———. 1970. *Rudyard Kipling: Stories and Poems.* Edited by Roger Lancelyn Green. London: Dent.

———. 1971. "Letter to Mrs. F. C. Burton." 1887. Reprinted in *Kipling: The Critical Heritage,* edited by Roger Lancelyn Green. London: Routledge.

———. 1987. *Debits and Credits.* 1926. Reprint, Harmondsworth: Penguin.

———. 1989. *Rudyard Kipling: Selected Stories.* Edited by Sandra Kemp. London: Dent.

———. 1990. *Something of Myself and Other Autobiographical Writings.* Edited by Thomas Pinney. Cambridge: Cambridge University Press.

Kübler-Ross, Elizabeth. 1984. "A Philosophy for Living and Dying." *Listener,* 3 May, 8.

Lewis, C. S. 1969. *Selected Literary Essays.* Cambridge: Cambridge University Press.

Lilly, W. S. 1900. "The Parlous State of England." *The Nineteenth Century* 47 (April).

Mackail, J. W. 1929. *The Lesson of Imperial Rome.* London: John Murray.

———. 1934. *Latin Literature.* 1895. Reprint, London: John Murray.

Male, Émile. 1958. *The Gothic Image.* Translated by Nora Hussey. 1913. Reprint, New York: Harper and Row.

Mallet, Philip, ed. 1989. *Kipling Considered.* London: Macmillan.

Mardrus, J. C., and Powys Mathers. 1958. *The Book of the Thousand Nights and One Night.* 4 vols. London: The Folio Society.

Marwick, Arthur. 1967. *The Deluge.* 1965. Reprint, Harmondsworth: Penguin.

Mason, Philip. 1975. *Kipling: The Glass, the Shadow, and the Fire.* London: Jonathan Cape.

McBratney, J. 1990. "Lovers Beyond the Pale: Images of Women in Kipling's Tales of Miscegenation." *Works and Days* 8 (spring): 17–36.

McKenzie, J. M. 1984. *Propaganda and Empire.* Manchester: Manchester University Press.

Merriman, H. S. 1966. *Young Mistley.* 1888. Reprint, London: Cassell.

Mohanty, S. P. 1991. "Drawing the Color Line: Kipling and Culture of Colonial Rule." In *The Bounds of Race: Perspectives in Hegemony and Resistance,* edited by Dominick La Canna. Ithaca: Cornell University Press.

Moore-Gilbert, B. 1986. *Kipling and "Orientalism."* London: Croom Helm.

Morris, A. J. 1984. *The Scaremongers: The Advocacy of War, 1890–1914.* London: Routledge and Kegan Paul.

Morris, James. 1979. *Heaven's Command: An Imperial Progress.* 1973. Reprint, Harmondsworth: Penguin.

Nordau, Max. *Degeneration.* London: Heinemann, 1895. Quoted in R. K. R. Thornton, *The Decadent Dilemma* (London: Routledge, 1983), 300.

Noyes, Alfred. 1971. Review of *Puck of Pook's Hill,* by Rudyard Kipling. *The Bookman* 31 (1906). Reprinted in *Kipling: The Critical Heritage,* edited by R. L. Green. London: Routledge and Kegan Paul.

O'Day, Alan, ed. 1979. *The Edwardian Age: Conflict and Stability.* London: Macmillan.

Orel, H., ed. 1989. *Critical Essays on Rudyard Kipling.* Boston: G. K. Hall.

Orwell, George. 1966. "Rudyard Kipling." In *Collected Essays.* 1945. Reprint, London: Mercury.

Paffard, Mark. 1989. *Kipling's Indian Fiction.* London: Macmillan.

Parry, A. 1992. *The Poetry of Rudyard Kipling.* Buckingham and Philadelphia: Open University Press.

Parry, B. 1987. "Problems in Current Theories of Colonial Discourse." *Oxford Literary Review* 9, nos. 1 and 2.

Phillips, G. 1979. *The Diehards: Aristocratic Society and Politics in Edwardian England.* Cambridge: Harvard University Press.

Pipes, Richard. 1994. *Communism: The Vanished Specter.* Oxford: Oxford University Press.

Quennell, Peter. 1969. *Shakespeare: The Poet and His Background.* 1963. Reprint, Harmondsworth: Penguin.

Ross, E. K. 1984. "A Philosophy for Living and Dying." *Listener,* 3 May, 8.

Runciman, Steven. 1965. *A History of the Crusades.* 3 vols. Harmondsworth: Penguin.

Russell, Bertrand. 1971. *A History of Western Philosophy.* 1945. London: Allen & Unwin.

Rutherford, A., ed. 1964. *Kipling's Mind and Art.* London: Oliver and Boyd.

Said, E. 1978. *Orientalism.* London: Penguin.

Saintsbury, George. 1917. *A History of the French Novel to the Close of the Nineteenth Century.* Vol. 1. London: Macmillan.

Sandison, A. 1967. *The Wheel of Empire.* London: Macmillan.

Searle, G. 1978. *The Quest for National Efficiency.* Oxford: Basil Blackwell.

Shaw, George Bernard. 1986. *Major Critical Essays.* Harmondsworth: Penguin.

Singhal, D. P. 1983. *A History of the Indian People.* London: Methuen.

Stewart, J. I. M. 1966. *Rudyard Kipling.* London: Victor Gollancz.

Bibliography

Stokes, E. 1960. *The Political Ideas of English Imperialism.* Oxford: Oxford University Press.

Strickland, Agnes. 1904. *The Life of Queen Elizabeth.* London: Hutchinson.

Sullivan, Zohreh T. 1984. "Kipling the Nightwalker." *Modern Fiction Studies* 30, no. 2:217–35.

———. 1993. *Narratives of Empire: The Fictions of Rudyard Kipling.* Cambridge: Cambridge University Press.

Swinnerton, Frank. 1966. Introduction to *Young Mistley,* by Henry Seton Merriman. 1888. Reprint, London: Cassell.

Tanner, J. R., E. V. Previté, and Z. N. Brook, eds. 1927. *The Cambridge Medieval History.* Vol. 6. Cambridge: Cambridge University Press.

Thornton, R. K. R. 1983. *The Decadent Dilemma.* London: Edwin Arnold.

Tompkins, J. M. S. 1965. *The Art of Rudyard Kipling.* 1959. Reprint, London: Methuen.

Wilson, Angus. 1977. *The Strange Ride of Rudyard Kipling.* London: Secker and Warburg.

Woodruff, Philip. 1953. *The Founders.* Vol. 1 of *The Men Who Ruled India.* London: Jonathan Cape.

———. 1954. *The Guardians.* Vol. 2 of *The Men Who Ruled India.* London: Jonathan Cape.

Index

Al Kamil (sultan of Egypt), 107–8
Alphonso the Wise (king of Castile), 114
Al Raschid, Haroun, 107
Amery, Leo, 62
Arabian Nights, The, 107
Arendt, Hannah, 18
Aristotle, 110, 113
astrology, 70, 111
Averroës (Ibn Rushd), 110

Bacon, Roger, 111
Balfour, Arthur, 63
banal subjects, later-nineteenth-century interest in, 26
Bayley, John, 13
Belloc, Hilaire, 22
Benjamin, Walter, 18
Bernard, St., 104
Bhabha, Homi, 15
Bodelsen, C. A., 100–101
Bonaventure, St., 111
Booth, "General" William, 23
Browning, Robert, 81, 93

Calvinism, 79–80
Carthage, parallels between Edwardian Britain and, 22
Chamberlain, Joseph, 62
Charles I (king of England), 64
Chesterton, G. K., 21–22, 24, 29
cold iron, symbolism of, 48–52
Conrad, Joseph, 22, 32
contemporary model of Kipling criticism, the, 15–17

Cook, Nora, 14, 16
Corbet, Richard, 64

Dangerfield, George, 63
Dante, 108, 111
Doyle, Sir Arthur Conan, 22
Drake, Sir Francis, 71–72
Drummond of Hawthornden, William, 121

Eliade, Mircea, 50, 97
Elizabeth I (queen of England), 53–54
Ellis, John M., 28
evolutionary reversion, 31
Ewing, Juliana Horatia, 89–90

Flaubert, Gustave, 26
Foucault, Michel, 15
Frederick II (Holy Roman Emperor), 108
Freeman, E. A., 38
Freemasonry, 87–88
Fuller, Thomas, 120

Gehazi, 35
Gibbon, Edward, 18–19
Gilbert, Eliot L., 13
gnosis, 85, 91, 93, 99
Golding, William, 58
Goncourt, Edmond de, 26
Goncourt, Jules de, 26
Grant, Michael, 93
Green, J. R., 38, 73

Haggard, Sir Henry Rider, 23
Hanuman, 34

Index

Hardy, Thomas, 23
Harold II (king of England), 73
Henley, W. E., 26
Henry I (king of England), 73–74
historical assumptions of recent Kipling criticism, 17–21
Hobshawm, Eric, 18
Hobson, J. A., 15, 21–22
homosocial bonding, 31

Indian Mutiny, the, 19–20
Islam, Shamsul, 47

Jews, the, 45–46, 76–78, 81–82
Joinville, Jean, lord of, 114–18
Jonson, Ben, 120–25

Kemp, Sandra, 14
Kipling, Rudyard: anger over political situation, 1906–14, 62; art, view on, 25–27; effect of First World War on, 60; imaginative magnanimity, 83; interest in a spiritual aristocracy, 91; loyalty, problem of finding a worthy object of, 65; mental image of the British Empire, 102–3; Radical Right and, 72–73; reconciliation of art and intellectualism, 127; redemption theme in works of, 83; reticence, 24; scholarly interests in late work, 120. Works: "The Eye of Allah," 100–119; "The House Surgeon," 16, 76–82; *Life's Handicap,* 77; *Limits and Renewals,* 83–99; "The Mark of the Beast," 30–36; "Proofs of Holy Writ," 120–27; *Puck of Pook's Hill,* 37–46; *Rewards and Fairies,* 47–75.
Kübler-Ross, Elizabeth, 56

Lang, Andrew, 30
Lawrence, D. H., 41, 72–73
Lenin, V. I., 15
Lewis, C. S., 105
Lewis, Lisa, 101
liberal intellectuals, 63–64
Louis IX (St. Louis, king of France), 115, 117–18
Lull, Raymond, 104

MacKail, J. W., 39

Male, Emile, 104
Mallet, Phillip, 13
Mason, Philip, 47–48
McBratney, J., 14, 16
Mendelssohn, Moses, 78
Merriman, Henry Seton, 24
Milner, Lord Alfred, 59, 62
Mithraism, 43–44
Mogul Empire, 20–21
Mohanty, S. P., 14, 16
Moore, George, 26
Moravian Brethren, the, 66

Napoleon I (emperor of France), 67, 69
national efficiency, 59
Nietzsche, Friedrich Wilhelm, 45
Nordau, Max, 22–23
Noyes, Alfred, 22

O'Day, Alan, 63
Oliphant, Margaret, 28, 30
Orwell, George, 62
Other, the, 15, 16, 31
Outram, Sir James, 19

Paffard, Mark, 14, 26
Paul, St., 69, 92, 94–99
pessimism in the 1890s and the Edwardian era, 22–24
phantoms of the living, 80
Pinney, Thomas, 24
Pipes, Richard, 17
political correctness, 16
pre-Socratic philosophers, 84–85

racial theories of history, 38–39
reconciliation of the weak and defeated, 45
Ricketts, Harry, 13
Robin Goodfellow, theme of, 50
Rome, parallels between British Empire and, 37
Rosebery, Lord, 59

Said, Edward, 14, 20
Saintsbury, George, 114–15, 120
Scandinavian legend, 40–41, 49, 51–52, 64–65
Scotti, Michael, 111
Seneca Indians, 66–67
Shakespeare, William, 26, 120–25

Index

Shakespearian mind, the, 126
Sharpe, William, 30
Shaw, George Bernard, 22–23
Singhal, D. P., 20
Stewart, J. I. M., 47
Strickland, Agnes, 54
Sullivan, Zohreh T., 14, 15–18, 29
Sultanate of Delhi, 21

Tacitus, 38, 44
Talleyrand (-Perigord), Charles-Maurice de, 68–69
Thucydides, 18–19

Tompkins, J. M. S., 37, 47, 100, 102
Tories of the Edwardian era, 59, 62, 71, 75
Torrigiano, Pietro, 54
Treitschke, Heinrich von, 38
Trevelyan, G. M., 47

Washington, George, 67
Weland, 40, 42
Wilson, Angus, 37, 53, 80
Woodruff, Philip, 19

Zam-Zammah (the Gun in *Kim*), 20